Praise for One Mother to Another

"Every mother should have a best friend to give her the *real* lowdown on what motherhood is like. Melissa Mowry is that friend, and this book is that lowdown."

—Jill Smokler, *New York Times* bestselling author of *Confessions of a Scary Mommy* and founder of scarymommy.com

"In a saturated world of parenting books, Melissa's writing is a breath of fresh air. She brings humor and humility into her storytelling, and you will find yourself nodding in solidarity with her experiences and exclaiming, 'Me too!' "

—Alison Lee, co-editor of *Multiples Illuminated: A Collection of Stories and Advice From Parents of Twins, Triplets and More*

"Melissa Mowry's *One Mother to Another* reminds me of conversations I have with my candid, funny, vulnerable mom friends—the stories that save me from the sometimes overwhelming stress of parenting."

—Ann Imig, founder of the award-winning production LISTEN TO YOUR MOTHER

"Melissa Mowry writes the truth about motherhood like she's talking to a friend. A friend who can handle the sweet moments, the quiet moments, and the dirtiest moments. (No, this isn't mommy porn, I'm talking about dirty diapers, people! Sheesh.) If you need a friend to tell you the truth, then *One Mother to Another* is the book for you."

—Jen Mann, *New York Times* bestselling author of *People I Want to Punch in the Throat: Competitive Crafters, Drop-Off Despots, and Other Suburban Scourges*

"Melissa Mowry writes, 'Time has a way of spackling over the hard parts. . . . ' And she's right. As mothers over time, we reminisce about our children with a different lens. The beauty here is that Mowry shines light on all of motherhood: the good, the hard, and the blowout diaper. A lovely, honest, real look at motherhood from a down-to-earth mom, and a talented writer. Read this book for the straight scoop on motherhood—not to scare you, but to see its full beauty. Motherhood is hard, it's scary, it's overwhelming, but it's the best thing you'll ever do, and so worth it. Just ask Mowry: she'll tell you, from one mother to another."

—Jenny Kanevsky, author of *Chosen Quarry*

"You can't help but love Melissa Mowry. She is us, we are her, and we're all screwed."

—Jessica Ziegler, award-winning author of *Science of Parenthood*

"*One Mother to Another* reads less like a book and more like every conversation you've ever had with a best friend—the ones where you say what you mean without any fear of "bad mom" judgment, the ones you know your husband and mother-in-law will never hear about—her raw honesty as fresh and unassuming as it is endearing. Melissa's stories will draw you in, but her witty voice and lovely prose will keep you engaged to the end. "*One Mother To Another: This is Just Between Us*" is the book I wish someone had given me while I was in the trenches, desperate for a voice of camaraderie, and it will be the book I give to any new moms in my tribe in the future."

—Tori Grenz, editor, Mamalode.com

"Melissa has a fresh and honest voice that makes her stories feel so grounded and real. While reading her essays, it was easy for me to imagine that her experiences are mine, because in many ways they are. Relatable, funny and insightful, this is the book every mother should have on her nightstand."

—Sarah Cottrell, *Bangor Daily News*

One Mother to Another: This Is Just Between Us

Melissa Mowry

ISBN: 0692701818
ISBN 13: 9780692701812

For Chase and Sam. You are my life's best story.

Table of Contents

"Perhaps it takes courage to raise children..."

—John Steinbeck, *East of Eden*

Preface

I will never forget the way I felt in that moment.

The door clicked closed behind my husband, off to work, off to a world that didn't include me. It was the first day I'd be completely alone with our two-week-old son and I was far from ready. Just moments before, I'd felt a hand between my shoulder blades as I stood at the changing table where our infant son lay wriggling and shrieking. "I have to leave now," my husband had said gently, like a member of the bomb squad handling an explosive that's about to detonate.

My eyes immediately filled. "Seriously?" I asked with anger, hot tears sliding down my face and bleeding into the fabric of my oversized tee shirt. I might have been the more surprised of the two of us to find myself sobbing without any warning. "I had no idea you were leaving already. I didn't even get to shower," I said, an accusation. I needed a scapegoat, someone to absorb my anger and frustration and the overwhelming fear of being alone for nine long hours trapped in a tiny apartment with an infant I didn't yet understand.

"I'm really sorry, but I have a meeting that I'm already running late for," he explained before kissing us both and making for the door like a little kid bursting onto the playground at recess.

And then the doorknob turned and the car disappeared around the corner and I felt more alone than I could ever remember feeling. It was early March and the snow was piled up high around our driveway; I knew there would be no wasting an hour pushing the stroller or lying on the grass under the tree in the side yard. Basically, I was trapped; trapped inside an apartment that measured less than ten paces across with a mountain of laundry on the bedroom floor and two loads of dishes in the sink and an infant whose angry little suck made my nipples bleed through my shirt.

I was alone. And it was absolutely terrifying.

Though it's been years since that day, I doubt I will ever forget how it felt to be a brand new mom standing alone in my kitchen, watching my only lifeline float off to his morning meeting. That feeling—that huge, crushing, swallow-me-whole feeling—is exactly the reason I decided to write this book. It's not because I want to see my name on the shelf in Barnes & Noble or because I have a list of credentials that in any way qualifies me to write a book about being a parent. I don't—I'm probably the farthest thing from an expert that you could imagine. All I am is a fellow mother who understands that feeling you have on the first day alone with a screaming infant; or the day you venture out into the world and you have no idea how to transfer your baby from inside the car to inside the grocery store; or the random Tuesday three years in when nothing goes according to plan and you feel exactly like you did on day one.

That feeling is the reason I wrote this book.

At 26 when I had Chase, my first baby, I was one of the first of my friends to join the ranks of motherhood. I knew I wouldn't be on the receiving end of that invaluable parenting wisdom that comes from a close girlfriend over a glass of wine when the husbands are out of earshot. Though I'm a social person, I made mom friends slowly and was surprised at how difficult and, sometimes, awkward it was to do so as an adult. I craved connection with anyone who understood this new life into which I'd been violently thrust and I had very little idea how to soothe the feeling of being utterly alone.

So I did what so many of us do to combat loneliness these days: I took to the solace of the Internet.

Starting a WordPress blog was free and afforded me a place to publish my thoughts almost as quickly as they jumped out of my mind and onto the screen. The first post I published was called "Mom Guilt: There's Pretty Much Always Something You Should Feel Bad About." It was a tongue-in-cheek commentary on how, as soon as I became a mother, I felt guilty about every little thing under the sun, up to and including the hostility I harbored for people who asked me any kind of baby-related question during the third trimester and the fact that I almost never did tummy time with my infant.

I shared it on my personal Facebook page and an unexpected thing happened: a few other moms I knew from my teaching days chimed in, saying they felt the same way I did. Here I was pouring my thoughts onto the page as a form of therapy, having no idea that anyone else felt the way I had for the past four months and suddenly other moms were saying they understood.

It was intoxicating.

I kept writing.

I filled up my friends' News Feeds with stories about my struggle to breastfeed, how I sometimes missed the twosome my husband and I were before our son was born, the profoundly gut-wrenching experience of miscarrying our first baby. I was honest, sometimes brutally so; I emotionally undressed myself time and again for the Internet and was rewarded in kind with other moms' honesty.

For many months it was just another one of the tiny mom blogs occupying little online space, but to me it was a lifeline. If I had a bad day, all I had to do was cast my net into the proverbial waters and I'd pull it back with a handful of comments from other moms who knew exactly what I was feeling. We commiserated about teething and lack of sleep. I asked for lots of advice. Those who were more knowledgeable than me shared their wisdom, *one mother to another*. It was a beautiful thing.

Then one day, a little over a year into this blogging venture and just two short months into being a second-time mom, I did a completely insane thing and decided to write a book. I couldn't even get my laundry folded within four days of it exiting the dryer and I was somehow ready to tackle this massive undertaking. I had zero qualifications, no idea if anyone would take me seriously and nothing motivating me but that feeling I had the day my husband drove off to work and left me alone with our terrifying little stranger. It didn't make any sense, but it felt like something I had to do.

All that to say, if you're looking for a book written by an expert who is well-versed in the latest research on baby-wearing or who knows the best method for getting an infant to sleep through the night then this book will be a surefire disappointment. There are loads of great books on the market that deal with the ins and outs of childrearing if you're in the market for concrete, factual answers. But if you want to read something from another mom who is still learning the ropes right alongside you, who appreciates the gift of motherhood but sometimes forgets to be grateful, who loves her children fiercely but doesn't always love being a mom, then you've stumbled upon the right book.

This book is what I like to call a "fill in the gaps book," which is to say that it attempts to fill in the gaps of knowledge about what motherhood is really like that other books don't touch on quite as much. It's less about the physical side of motherhood (though there's some of that, too) and more about the emotional side, which I think is just as important when you're in the trenches, as I am right now.

I can promise you little except total honesty. I won't sugarcoat motherhood, but I won't lose sight of how awesome and absolutely worth it, it is. All I can tell you with absolute certainty is that motherhood is a delicate balance and the pendulum swings from one extreme to another with each minute that passes. Sometimes it's beautiful and perfect and sometimes it's messy and lonely and terrifying and sometimes it's all those things in the exact same second. The key is learning to thrive in the gray area and knowing you're doing the best you can with what you've got at that moment.

As the name implies, this book is more about the kind of admissions whispered between girlfriends than about the things we confess right out loud. It's about coming to terms with breaking all the rules we said we'd follow before actually having children, about grappling with the lightning-quick shift between reveling in their proximity and wanting to be as far away from them as possible. More than anything, it's about learning to accept the kind of mothers we've become, even if they're nothing like the kind we envisioned we'd be at the beginning.

For the record, I'm still learning that one, too.

From one mother to another,

Melissa

The Sometimes Mom

Sometimes I feed my son organic fruit smoothies that I make lovingly in my blender; sometimes he eats store brand Fruit Loops covered in artificial flavors that are stuck to my unwashed floor.

Sometimes I wake up before my son, shower and dress in something other than sweatpants, looking halfway respectable if I should happen to leave the confines of my house; sometimes I opt for elastic waist pants, use deodorant in lieu of a shower and cancel any plans that require me to walk past the front porch.

Sometimes I get down on the floor and assemble block towers and read books and sing the Itsy Bitsy Spider; sometimes I can't be bothered because I'm just so bored with entertaining a baby for 10 hours a day.

Sometimes I hustle upstairs and grab my son from his crib the minute I hear him stirring from his nap; sometimes, I just want three more minutes of peace, so I let him wait it out while I sit at the kitchen table doing absolutely nothing.

Sometimes, when my husband comes home after work, the dishwasher and sink are empty, the floor is vacuumed and dinner is already in the oven; sometimes the sink and dishwasher are overflowing to Leaning Tower proportions, the floor is full of crushed-up Goldfish and I beg him to please order takeout—despite it not being in the budget—so I don't have to cook one more damned meal this week.

Sometimes I put my phone away and focus my attention completely on my son; sometimes I get caught up in reading articles about being a good mom while I ignore my child altogether.

Sometimes I put my son down for a nap and I'm scarily productive; sometimes I haul my son into bed with me and we nap for a blissfully unproductive two hours, waking up to a pile of unfinished to-dos.

Sometimes I feel beyond lucky that I get to stay home with my son everyday; sometimes I wish someone needed me for something, *anything,* more pressing than cutting his food into tiny, bite-sized pieces or unearthing a block that's stuck under the coffee table.

Sometimes I don't give a damn what every other mom is doing because I'm confident in my own brand of motherhood; sometimes I can't help but compare my thighs to the ones on the skinnier mom in the checkout line or get jealous over the vacation to Jamaica another family can afford that we cannot.

I am a mother of contradictions. At any given moment, I am a different mother to my son than I was just moments before. I am flawed and inconsistent, capable and inept, a million different colors splashed on the same canvas.

But even in my moments of ineptitude, of laziness, of just plain not-getting-it-right, I am always a good mother. And so are you. Even if your kid eats red dye #40 and you find a

Facebook trending topic more interesting than your baby and you lose your temper because someone walked in on you in the bathroom for the tenth time today. Even then, you're still a good mom; you're just not a perfect one.

But everyone gets it perfectly right. Sometimes.

Five Senses

My husband emerges from the walk-in closet, sporting a pair of wrinkled green dress pants and a collared shirt that can only be described as candy apple red.

"Does this match?" he asks with a note of uncertainty, standing before me like a *What Not to Wear* contestant in front of the 360-degree mirror.

I respond with as much seriousness as I can manage to the very adorable grown man wearing Christmas colors in June. "No, not at all," I tell him charitably as I pick through his side of the closet and wonder if he'd have gone into work in that outfit had I still been asleep in bed. "I'll help you find something."

Though my husband is no fashion mogul, his faux pas has more to do with genetics than a blatant disregard for the reigning trends in menswear. Like his father, Adam was born colorblind. Which, contrary to popular belief, doesn't always translate into seeing the world solely in black and white.

In my husband's case, it's more like missing a handful of the more obscure colors from the box of 96 Crayolas—the ones like Cerulean and Burnt Sienna that most fully-sighted people probably couldn't pick out of a lineup. The way he views certain shades is much different than the way I see them; to him, that candy apple red shirt is softer, more palatable, the Army green bordering on a much more sensible brown.

Which is sort of how I view life before motherhood: not a crayon box with a gaping hole where one of the colors should be, but more like a muted version of the full set.

When you become a mother, it's like all the senses instantly take on a heightened quality, as if you never knew what it was like to truly *feel* before children. I'm not talking about the sun shining brighter and birds singing louder, like suddenly motherhood transforms you into Mary Poppins floating around with a magic umbrella. I mean it on a more basic level: the day-to-day stuff that never seemed important until the minute the doctors placed a warm, slimy newborn on your chest.

Though you once sort of liked the smell of lilacs or kind of preferred the scent of Chanel to Marc Jacobs, you now cannot go two minutes without inhaling your new baby's milky skin or the top of his downy little head—the instinct is as innate as breathing. As he gets older, you learn to discern his certain brand of freshly soiled diaper from those of the other 25 toddlers at music class, quickly ferrying him off to the nearest changing table. When your teenage son saturates the car with the odor of too much Axe Body Spray, you won't know whether your eyes are filling because of the overwhelming aroma or because your little boy—the one that always smelled like dirt and sweat and his own unique scent— is no longer a little boy at all.

You will realize that, before becoming a mother, you never really knew what it felt like to be touched. To constantly have a pair of little hands winding around your legs, a finger poking at your midsection asking too many questions about why it's so soft, a warm little body seeking solace in your too-small bed after a nightmare. You will, at certain times, soak up the proximity, knowing it won't last forever and, at others, wish away the never-ending assault on your personal space, begging for just two minutes to pee alone.

Though you probably enjoyed food in a less-hurried fashion before children, the taste of a good meal suddenly becomes a precious novelty—especially when you don't have to eat it directly over the garbage can. You learn to cultivate (and appreciate) a slightly less refined palate—a handful of stale Goldfish, the crust of a half-eaten sandwich, the dregs of a bowl of cereal your toddler didn't finish before sprinting off to watch Mickey Mouse Clubhouse. And after nine months of pregnancy, nothing could ever taste as perfect as a cold beer, a sandwich piled with deli meat or a tub of cookie dough. (Except maybe that chocolate that you keep stashed in the bathroom for emergencies.)

All at once, you can hear everything within a 5-mile radius, certain you can pick out the sound of your child crying even when the shower is on or the vacuum is running. You can differentiate between the pitch of your toddler's whiny cry when another kid at the playground takes his toy and the full-blown scream when he falls off the monkey bars. At night, you quietly curse the noises of your still-active neighborhood—the dog that won't stop barking outside your sleeping baby's window, the fireworks going off at 10:00 p.m., the plow that keeps scraping its way down your snow-filled street. And when your house is finally empty after many years of noise and chaos, the sound of silence is deafening.

From that first glimpse of the tiny lentil on the ultrasound, there is the immediate realization that you had no idea what a gift the sense of sight was until you became someone's mother. Even if, before children, you hiked through caves in Yucatan or watched sunsets bleed into the Sonoma skyline, nothing will ever compare to the sight of your son running full-force into your arms after a day at daycare, of your daughter winding her hair around her finger, exactly the way you do. The capacity to bear witness to your child's gradual growth becomes your body's single greatest ability.

There are days when motherhood is an all-consuming, neuron-frying sensory overload. There are times when it feels like there are too many colors packed in the box of Crayolas and I wish for something simpler, less overwhelming. But I'd take this craziness over the considerably duller version of my "before" life any day. All I have to do is look at my adorably mismatched husband to remember an important truth: not everyone is lucky enough to experience life in full color.

A Letter to Myself As a New Mother

Dear Me,

As you sit there holding your brand new baby, there are so many things I want you to know about what lies ahead for you. Some of those things have yet to transpire—I am still learning about motherhood with every day that passes—but much of this advice will make your first year a little bit smoother. Take it to heart now.

First of all, you are in the hardest stage right at this moment; it will get easier with each day you make it through in one piece. There will be days when you wonder why you wished for parenthood so fervently because it has changed every single thing about your life as you knew it. Motherhood will intimidate you and fill you with confidence; it will depress you and make you happier than you ever imagined possible. Everything you feel right now is normal. Possibly insane, but normal. With time, the intensity of your hormones will wear off and you will remember what it's like to be you— the you that occasionally slept more than two hours straight and didn't cry every time someone says she likes the color of your shirt. Don't worry if you don't have it all figured out from day one; very few moms do. Just remember: this stage is hard, but it will only get easier from here.

I see you sitting in your mommy and me class, staring enviously at the women with babies older than yours. You note how casual their movements are, how practiced they seem at carrying on a conversation while breastfeeding or efficiently diapering their babies. Meanwhile you fumble and sweat, accidentally expose your nipple to the whole group and use an entire package of wipes for one dirty diaper. I promise you will get the hang of it and, someday soon, you will be that woman whom another mom watches with jealous admiration. There's no shame in being green. Even the moms who make it look easy had to start somewhere.

You and Adam are both new to this. Cut each other some slack. He can't read your mind and he doesn't know whether you're crying because the baby rolled over for the first time or because he accidentally bought off-brand granola bars. He wants to help you any way he can, but he's not always sure what you need. Let him help you and then give him the freedom and autonomy to parent your children in his own way without you second-guessing him at every turn. No, he won't always do things the way you would, but that's OK. In fact, it's great. It means that he and your son will form a bond that's separate and unique from the one you have with him.

Motherhood is lonely, sometimes overwhelmingly so. Get out there and find your people: other moms who understand the unbelievably hard transition you are going through at this moment. That woman in the park with the really nice stroller and the son who is about the same age as yours? Talk to her. Chances are she's looking for a friend too. I promise, she won't turn you down if you ask for her number. She might just prove to be the person who saves you from yourself. Or maybe she won't and you'll meet up once and realize it's not going to work out. That happens a few times, too. But you'll never find your tribe unless you put yourself out there and make the first move.

Trust your instincts. They are the greatest tools at your disposal. As a new mother, you'll be constantly fielding advice from everyone you know (and often total strangers) about the best way to raise your children. Some of their advice will be sound, possibly even helpful. But your own instincts should trump theirs at every turn. You won't always know what's best—there's a lot of trial and error involved in being a mother—but if you have a feeling in your gut, don't ignore it. You're much more likely to regret the outcome if you disregard what your gut is telling you than if you take a risk and trust yourself.

Go easy on your body. I know you feel uncomfortable in it right now, but it deserves some grace. It just carried a human life for nine months and then pushed that human out into the world. No, it doesn't quite look like the body you used to know, but it's not supposed to right away. Or maybe ever. When you're feeling discouraged or even disgusted by it, remember all that it has done for you.

Try not to feel guilty about so many things. I promise you, you are not doing everything wrong. Even if you screw up (which you will) your son will forgive you. Feeling guilty all the time will not make you a better mom any more than singing in the shower every day will give you a better voice; you're just wasting the precious time during which you could be enjoying your son's childhood. Lay off the guilt and know that you are doing absolutely all you can to give Chase the best life possible.

You will not love every minute, or even every day, of being a mother. That's normal. I doubt there are mothers out there who do. Some parts of motherhood are just not enjoyable by nature, like public tantrums and getting someone else's fecal matter wiped on you. When you're not loving it, take a deep breath, allow yourself some time to regroup, then come back and commence loving the hell out of your child. (And if you start to feel guilty about it, refer to the previous paragraph.)

Be kind to your fellow mother. Motherhood is hard enough without moms tearing each other down over the decision to co-sleep or bottle feed or use pacifiers. When you bear witness to another mom's parenting and your first instinct is to judge, keep in mind that you don't know the whole story; there might be circumstances at play of which you are completely unaware. Even if you do know the whole story, that other mom's decision to raise her children in a certain way has absolutely nothing to do with you. Consider it only your business to be kind to other moms, to exercise compassion and understanding. You never know when you'll need that kindness extended to you. Believe me: karma is a real thing.

I'm sure you're overwhelmed already and I've given you enough to chew on right now. Even if you forget everything I've said here, remember this: you are a good mother who is doing the best she can. The rest is just details.

Love,

You

Aftermath

"Unfortunately, I'm not seeing a heartbeat."

The technician gives me her best sympathetic face and my hands ball in my paper gown, willing her to leave before my fist lands between her perfectly plucked eyebrows. The feeling of anger surprises me as it wells up in me quick and strong, but there's no denying how inappropriate it seems.

I wait until she shuts the door with a quiet click and then fold at the waist, choking out sobs that can surely be heard through the thin walls. I picture the women on the other side of those walls clutching their swollen bellies and shifting uncomfortably on the examination table, politely ignoring the wounded sounds emanating from the next room. In the chair beside me, my husband buries his head in his hands. I can't look at him because his pain guts me. I pretend I'm alone in the room.

Though I haven't seen myself in a mirror, I know I'm an ugly crier and I avoid the receptionist's eyes as she processes the last of my paperwork before we exit the office. I look young—much younger than my almost 26 years—and I absently wonder if she thinks I've just received news of an unplanned pregnancy. I hate her for no logical reason and rip the receipt from her hand when she offers it across the desk.

In the car, I am alone and it is 11:30 a.m. I sent Adam back to work, knowing I couldn't juggle the weight of two people's grief. I begin to mentally calculate how much booze we have and where it is located in the house. Between trying to conceive and being pregnant, I haven't had a drink in ages—four months? five?—and the wine rack is nothing but twelve cavernous slots, filled with dust and stray cat hair. There's maybe a half a cocktail's worth of cherry vodka in the freezer and a bottle of warm champagne that we forgot to open last week at Easter when we announced the good news to our parents and siblings.

I make an split-second decision to procure more appealing booze and take a hard right into the liquor store parking lot. Consulting the rearview mirror, I wince, swiping a Dunkin Donuts napkin under my eyes where the mascara has pooled, dusting powder over my blotchy skin. I say a silent prayer of thanks that I know barely anyone in our new town and make quick work of the liquor store inventory. A bottle of sweet, cheap wine that goes down like juice and 750 mL of decent vodka that I'll combine with orange juice since there's been no reason for keeping good mixers in the house.

I feel almost happy as I pull into the driveway and heft my packages inside, the bottles clanking against each other in a satisfactory way. I uncork the wine, a sound I have almost-but-not-quite forgotten, and pour myself half—no three-quarters—of a wine glass into a fancy one we received for our wedding that I only use on special occasions. I feel like I should be toasting someone or something.

The alcohol goes to my head and I smile, but immediately feel guilty so I stop. My MacBook is open to a handful of pregnancy websites. I close my browser, open a blank document and begin to type a story about a woman who burns down her obstetrician's office and winds up in a mental institution. I abandon it after paragraph six because I'm suddenly angry again and a little bit buzzed and the words are starting to get away from me. But I'm not just angry now; I'm furious.

I refill my glass and stalk through the house, stuffing every baby-related item I can find into the complimentary tote bag I was given at my first doctor's appointment: tiny canvas shoes from the Gap—my first purchase after the positive home test result; the only two baby books I let myself buy—one for each of us—remembering how I gushed to the Barnes & Noble cashier after she asked if they were for me; the yellow polka dotted outfit my sister gave us, with a matching hat and a fuzzy blue blanket with the letters b-a-b-y imprinted on it; the pastel-colored plastic eggs with the miniature socks and pacifiers inside that we used to surprise our families at Easter brunch last week.

I think of all the things that I wanted to scream at the doctor's office, things that decent, respectable people don't shout in public places. Like why do crackheads and teenagers and women on birth control and people who don't even want kids get pregnant and get to keep their babies? How come it doesn't matter that I gave up drinking and eating spicy tuna rolls and taking Advil for headaches, swapping them for green smoothies at breakfast and organic chicken at dinner and pregnancy-safe Tylenol? Why doesn't it factor that I ran to stay in shape and lifted no more than the recommended 25 pounds and didn't eat sleeves of Oreos even when it sounded kind of appealing and no one would blame me? Why did I let myself believe I'd actually get to keep this baby even when I knew, deep down, that something was wrong?

I think of all the signs I tried to force away, to mask with excitement and preparation and thoughts of my husband holding our tiny baby and smiling the way he does when he's really, truly happy. But they were there, tangible and obvious and taunting, questioning why there was no morning sickness or cravings for pickles or mad dashes to the bathroom, just a slightly bigger bra cup size, mid-afternoon naps and a craving for peanut butter cup ice cream that couldn't be blamed on a baby. There were the tiny red dots on the toilet paper that became not so tiny after awhile and the 4 AM sweat-drenched wake ups every night since the positive test.

I'm worked up now and I decide I want to smash things, anything I can get my hands on. I start with the wine glass—finishing the contents first, of course—and hurl it at our bedroom door, which nicks the wood and fans a blanket of tiny shards across the beige carpet. Then I round up a handful of picture frames and hurl them against the back deck, watching the glass and wood splinter into a million tiny pieces, which I will have to clean up later, but not now. Into the woods go two potted Easter lilies from my mother-in-law and two dozen painted eggs in quick succession, though one wobbly throw has an egg hitting the doorframe above my head and landing at my feet. My arm hurts from throwing so hard and the urge to destroy has abandoned me as quickly as it came, leaving me hollow and tired and flimsy.

I take two Tylenol PMs and drift to sleep in front of a Leonardo DiCaprio movie, waking up to a black screen and no concept of how long I've been out. I finish off the night with a bottle of wine, three margaritas, two screwdrivers and one glass of champagne under my belt. The next day's hangover is enough to ensure I won't drink so recklessly and self-destructively again any time soon.

Everyone has a different statistic to comfort me. Thirty percent of pregnancies end in miscarriage, my obstetrician tells me. Fifty percent, says my primary care doctor. A friend cites 80%. Zero percent of me cares about those other women because my pain is real and immediate and so very fresh and I can't wrap my brain around theirs just yet. Is it too much to ask to just lick my wounds without everyone telling me about others who have been through it too? Can't I even be afforded the luxury of feeling horribly, unapologetically wrecked?

Friends from church and my mother-in-law send me cards and emails and texts with Bible verses and psalms and urge me to find the meaning in God's plan. I politely thank them for their kindness but leave out the part about how pissed I am at God for pulling the rug out from under me, how I think His plan royally sucks and that He is an Indian giver of the highest order. My mother-in-law says God doesn't work like that. My husband says I'm being pessimistic—good things and bad things aren't inherently intertwined—but I reserve my right to be skeptical. I am like a child of divorce, blaming myself irrationally but feeling the finger pointing at me all the same. Blame is the only thing that makes sense, so I grasp it tightly with both hands. I am being punished, but instead of deepening the pain, it comforts me.

The world streams around me, continuing with its ebb and flow. After several weeks, I stop acting like a sullen teenager and end my standoff with God, apologizing for acting horribly un-Christian and skipping church for three weeks. I know He forgives me, but I still feel like an asshole. My pregnant friends stay pregnant, carrying healthy babies that I will eventually fawn over and buy tiny outfits for, heralding their entrance into the world. I intentionally avoid the baby section in Target, keeping a wide berth so as not to lose my composure in a public place. Pregnant women sit across from me in my office at the daycare center, making small talk about due dates and possible names and their growing bellies. As more time passes, I notice that their due dates are later than mine would have been and it feels like a thousand internal paper cuts. The butcher knife feeling has subsided, but this is almost worse because it is unexpected and constant and I don't know how to make it stop.

Weeks pass and I throw myself into a new job that demands every ounce of my attention. We move into a blank slate home, needing badly to make something our own. I am busy and frenzied and without a moment in my day to pause—finally, happily distracted. But still there are those moments when I am alone in the car with nothing but the radio to distract me from my thoughts of the baby that was almost mine. The life we would have all had together that slipped through my fingertips, a life that seems absurd and impossible now.

I have no idea what the future holds for me. I don't know if this is just the first of many losses we will endure; if I'll never get the chance to carry another life inside me; if someday I'll be the mother to more kids than I can count on one hand. The only thing I know for certain is that I will never be the same again.

Misconceptions of Motherhood

efore I became a mother, I had a very fuzzy idea in my head of what a stay-at-home-mom was like. My own mother worked when I was growing up, so I'd never really encountered the stay-at-home-mom types. Most of my friends' moms worked full time too, and those that didn't always seemed busy—I was pretty sure they didn't actually *stay home*. To me, they were like snow leopards or the Aurora Borealis: I knew they existed, but without actual proof of what they were like in real life I was forced to fabricate a crudely rendered story in my own head.

I babysat a lot throughout my early 20s and one family in particular helped construct my frame of reference for who these unfamiliar stay-at-home-mom creatures were. This family lived in a modern, sprawling Cape-style home inside a gated community with a manicured lawn, two kids appropriately spaced three years apart and a golden retriever. (I know, a little too cliché.) The husband worked for a large international corporation and went on frequent business trips; the wife stayed home while the youngest attended the daycare center where I worked. More often than not she accompanied her husband on his corporate jet-setting, which was how I came to be involved.

I'd watch the kids while they scooted off to Santa Fe or Martha's Vineyard for several days, the wife modeling cocktail dress and strappy heel combinations for me as she packed her suitcase. On the granite countertop she'd leave meticulous instructions penned neatly on monogrammed stationery, detailing the types of organic snacks the kids should have packed in their lunchboxes, how to disarm the security system, directions for navigating their larger-than-life SUV from the two-car garage through their sleepy cul-de-sac to the elementary school down the street.

She always invited my husband to stay at the house with me when they were gone for whole weekends (even though we were married, I felt like the teenage babysitter sneaking her boyfriend in through the back door) and we'd sleep on their 400-thread-count sheets and use their expensive toiletries with designer names that certainly didn't hail from the drugstore shelves where I purchased my $7 bottles of Neutrogena face wash.

"If you need anything at all, call Jane from next door," she'd tell me. Jane had two kids of her own and also stayed home. In fact, I quickly learned that most of the neighborhood moms did. One was a personal trainer on the side, her basement transformed into a haven of yoga mats and pink rubber-capped dumbbells. Another mom sold Mary Kay. A third peddled Silpada jewelry, though, from the looks of her mini-mansion, she didn't need to sell anything at all.

So when I forgot an organically-stocked lunchbox on the counter, got poop on the carpet after neglecting to put a changing pad down on the floor and locked all three of us out of the house necessitating a call to Jane-from-next-door, I was sure I'd never be cut out for the stay-at-home-mom life. I simply didn't fit.

I was only a few years away from having kids of my own but that world seemed unreachable and entirely too put-together for someone who could barely get a meal on the table for two people before 8:00 p.m., never mind an entire family seven days a week. I'd never fit into their Zen, yoga pants-wearing tribe; I was much more likely to be the harried mom plunking three screaming kids down at daycare while dashing for the nearest exit.

Then, years later when I became a stay-at-home-mom, I discovered an unfathomable truth: that picture I had in my head? It wasn't even close to accurate. Sure, there are probably neighborhoods full of stay-at-home-moms who buy expensive designer face cream, use personal trainers and sleep on high thread count sheets, but I don't know any of them personally.

The moms I know have messy kitchens and six loads of dirty laundry waiting on their bedroom floors. They feed their kids pre-packaged snacks they can throw into the backseat of a moving car that they hope will keep running until the next paycheck hits the bank account. The moms I know haven't had an excuse to wear a cocktail dress since 1998 and a weekend getaway is a family trip to Costco. They lock themselves out of the house and forget lunchboxes on the counter and get poop on the carpet; their lives are messy and complicated and chaotic. Just like mine. And probably like that other mom's whose world seemed so perfect in the picture I fabricated in my head.

Every mother's life looks different, but I'd be hard-pressed now to find one that looks perfect, even in those gated-community mini-mansions with the golden retrievers frolicking around the landscaped yard. I'm sure that beneath the surface of that other mom's life, there were many hastily prepared meals that weren't even a little bit organic and more nights spent at home in sweatpants than out in cocktail dresses. If her life was a book, I read what amounted to a paragraph and convinced myself that was the whole story. Then, as I wrote my own story, I unfairly compared her one perfect paragraph to my whole book, finding myself coming up short. With the benefit of hindsight, I can see now that we were just different types of people doing the same hard job in our own ways. Neither of us was doing it right or wrong; all along, we were just writing different stories.

The Thing We Don't Talk About

Dear Son,

Now that you're learning to talk and your vocabulary is expanding by the day, I thought it was a good time to have a little chat about something. We share a lot of our lives with the world and, while that's all well and good, there's one thing that we should never talk about: *the art projects*.

You know the ones I'm referring to: the projects for which mommy spends 15 minutes laying out and carefully selecting the materials that you immediately crawl away from in search of an open toilet in which to play; the botched shaving cream sensory activity that you ingested within 2.5 seconds, provoking tears and warranting a frantic call to Poison Control; the chalk painting project that ended with you breaking every single piece of sidewalk chalk we own by throwing it to the floor and then ripping the paper in front of you to shreds.

No, we don't talk about those.

Mommy has a reputation to uphold. There are only so many filters I can apply to a photo to make it seem like you're having more fun doing the project than meeting Santa at the mall last Christmas. You've gotta work with me a little here, OK buddy?

You might not know this, but mommy spent the better part of your gestation on Pinterest frantically pinning age-appropriate projects that, admittedly, look much better when done with someone else's kids. These are things I thought would keep you happy for HOURS but that, in reality, hold your attention for mere seconds. All you seem to want to do is chew holes in the toilet paper and try to find the most dangerous cleaning products under the sink. What gives?

As a blogger, mommy has an important job: to give other moms hope that their children can realistically complete one successful project that requires an attention span of more than 13 seconds. We can't be dashing their hopes by talking about how you hate 87% of the activities mommy tries to do with you. We'd be letting them down.

So we have to step up our game a little bit. When I bring out the homemade play dough, try to really squish it between your fingers so mommy can snap a perfect close-up photo. When we blow the bubbles we made with dish soap and corn syrup, make sure you give a really cute, delighted smile so everyone knows that you love the home-made bubbles much more than the store-bought kind. And, whatever you do, make sure you don't dump the finger paint on the floor that mommy just washed two weeks ago.

Remember, this is our little secret, OK?

Love,

Mommy

When We're Not Together

When we're not together, I'm just another shopper selecting avocados in the produce section, an average customer making a deposit at the bank, an ordinary woman checking her hair in the bathroom mirror at a rest stop.

I'm not someone's mother—at least not noticeably—the evidence buried in the depths of my purse where an assortment of toy cars, baby wipes and half-eaten fruit bars take up residence next to my wallet and keys.

When we're not together, I bask in the simplicity of running errands without you, in the lightness of navigating parking lots and doctors' office waiting rooms unencumbered by diaper bags and car seats, free of clammy little hands holding mine or chubby legs locked around my midsection.

But I feel a tangible absence when no one approaches my cart to comment on your smile, when the man behind the deli counter who will happily twist his face into seemingly impossible expressions to make you laugh asks why I don't have my sidekick with me today.

When we're not together, I roll down the windows of daddy's fast little car that used to be mine and crank the stereo up to ear-bleeding decibels, luxuriating in the feeling of driving well over the speed limit. I hug the tight curves of the road and watch the needle on the speedometer inch upward, relishing the adrenaline rush that comes with driving the somewhat careless way I did before there was a piece of precious cargo strapped into the backseat.

But then I remember that with the music so loud I wouldn't be able to hear you singing in your adorably high-pitched voice, too young to know the words or care that you have an audience. That fast little car, I realize, would be speeding by the cars and trucks you excitedly name from the backseat, nothing but a blur in your little window to the world.

When we're not together, I try to convince myself that I'm still young enough to patronize trendy bars where the party doesn't start until well after I'm ordinarily at the tail end of a Netflix binge. I pretend that I belong there, clamoring for over-priced drinks with the fresh-out-of-college crowd, swaying on a packed dance floor in uncomfortably high heels to songs I no longer recognize.

Then I pull out my phone to check the time (*how is it only 9:30?*) and there's your toothy smile lighting up my screen, reminding me of what I'm missing when we're not together. In that moment, I secretly wish for nothing more than to be in the dark of your room rocking you to sleep, singing an off-key version of "Twinkle Twinkle Little Star" with your sweaty little head pressed into my chest.

When we're not together I can almost believe that I am some-one else entirely, a woman who doesn't spend her days clean-ing poop off her jeans while humming the theme song to Daniel Tiger's Neighborhood and her nights wrestling little bodies into pajamas and negotiating the number of bedtime books to be read. When we're not together, I am freer, less frazzled, more composed. I am simultaneously counting down the hours I can stay away and the minutes until I can come back to you.

It's true that I traded in a lot of my old life to become a mother—the freedom, the simplicity, the faster car and the loud-er music—all of which seems so tempting during the long days when we're together without a break from each other. But it's when we're apart that I realize just how much I'm missing out on when I'm away. Your absence reminds me that the coming home will always be infinitely better than the being gone.

Identity Crisis

"**M**ama."

At five months old, my son uttered that bright, beautiful word for the first time. Though it's been nearly a year and a half since that moment I still relish the feeling I got hearing it that day; remember the way he broke the word into two distinct syllables, how he drew out the "a" at the end. Everyone had told me that he'd say "dada" first. "Don't take offense. It's just easier for them to pronounce," they all said. But there he was with my name popping out of his mouth, the very first word that had ever crossed his lips. Talk about intoxicating stuff. If one's head could actually swell with pride, mine would've looked like a water balloon on the verge of bursting.

Since that day, he's said the word easily a thousand times, maybe more. He yells it when he wakes up in the morning and he wants me to come collect him from his crib. He calls it when he needs help reaching his milk across the kitchen table. He wails it when he falls on the pavement and needs my comfort.

He murmurs it when he's cuddled up to me, half-asleep on the couch at the end of a long day. It is used to refer to me far more than my given name; my girlfriends tack it on the end of a sentence instead of my real name, even my husband calls me mama more often than not. In so many ways, being a mama has taken over my identity. I am no longer Melissa, I am simply Mama: mother to Chase.

Can I let you in on a little secret though? There is nothing I cherish more in this world than that one little word.

Sometimes I think that's an unpopular opinion. Many of the women I know with children my son's age are sick to death of hearing that word come out of their kids' mouths. They crave some reprieve from its constant use and wish that anyone would remember they have an actual first name and are a person separate from their children's mother. They speak of the driven, determined, confident women they were pre-children and the exhausted, milk-stained, yoga pants-wearers they've become. They talk about feeling hemmed in by their new title, about wishing they were more than just Ethan's mom or the person that signs the permission slips and drives the carpool on Tuesdays. They wax poetic about the successful careers they left behind to pursue motherhood full-time; they miss the thrill of being needed for something more pressing than poking the straw through the juice box or mediating an argument about a broken LEGO tower. They want to be more than just a mama. I understand.

Sometimes I really miss the person I was before becoming a mama, too. I miss having a story more interesting to regale my husband with than a particularly gruesome blowout or the weird thing someone said to us in the grocery line. I miss achieving successes that have absolutely nothing to do with my children. I miss being able to eat a full meal using both hands. Parenthood is a monumental life change and it would be unrealistic to think that it doesn't come with some measure of growing pains.

But for some reason I still have not tired of hearing my son repeat that little word. Even when it's whined, even when it's wailed, even when it's yelled in anger—it still feels like a privilege to have it associated with me. Despite all the other aspirations I had for my life, I knew that becoming a mama would be my crowning achievement. The person I've become in the short time I've been a mother fits me better than the other identities I tried in the preceding 26 years. Being a mama makes sense in a way that so many other personas never did; instead of terrifying and panic-inducing, motherhood feels comfortable and confidence-inspiring, even during the times when I have exactly zero things figured out.

I spent most of my late teens and early-to-mid 20s feeling decidedly uncomfortable in my own skin. Not all that uncommon, I realize, but for me it was extreme. I was a harsh and exacting judge of my body, my personality, my life choices. I hurried through life stages, always thinking the next phase would be *my* time, my opportunity to finally figure it all out and become the person I really wanted to be. By the end of high school, I couldn't wait to move on to college, where I saw my future really unfolding. Then, once I reached college, I scrambled to graduate early so I could join the work force and prove myself to be a person of value. In the absence of a true identity, I struggled with a debilitating eating disorder. I figured, if nothing else, I would be defined by my thinness.

During those years, I saw other people with confidence and self-assurance seemingly oozing out of their pores and I'd try on their personalities, hoping one would fit. Of course they never did. Once I entered recovery for my eating disorder, I developed more confidence and started to hit my stride, but I had spent so many years defining myself by my weight that I had no idea who I really was once I came out on the other side. I jumped from job to job, never finding one that truly stirred up my passions or even one I could tolerate on a 9-5 basis for more than a calendar year. I was happy, but adrift.

When I got pregnant things quickly started to come into focus for me. I felt like the people in the Claritin commercial after the blurry film is ripped off the screen. I parted ways with my stressful job as the manager of a daycare center, which came with long, demanding hours and a 2-hour daily commute. I began working as a barista at a coffee shop where the pay was markedly less, but where I felt truly comfortable, sneaking bites of broken cookies as my belly swelled and customers began to count down the days right along with me.

Then Chase came. New motherhood was not all smiles and rainbows for me. It was lonely and isolating. There were many days when I felt like I'd never understand the little person I'd created and longed to return to the lower-stakes world of making cappuccinos for irritated businessmen. Still, I felt at ease in a way that I hadn't in such a long time. I had a spotty job history a mile long and no idea what I wanted to be when I grew up, but I was made to be someone's mother. I knew it beyond a shadow of a doubt.

I'm not saying I have it all figured out. That is so far from the truth it's laughable. Just the other day, my son cried for 45 minutes while I bounced and rocked him, cooed at and sung to him, all the while unaware that he was sitting in poop up to his shoulder blades. At times I feel like the applicant who lies on her resume and says she's proficient in Excel but can't even open a spreadsheet. Some days being a mother feels frighteningly easy.

Others, I feel wholly unqualified and wish I had an office door I could close so I could curl up in the fetal position under my desk.

I am a mama. It's the hardest, most demanding job I've ever had to date or will ever have in the future. All day long, I am needed in the most relentlessly incessant way: "Mama, I want this" or "Mama, don't do that." Yet I know I'm exactly where I should be. Even on the worst days, when my name is used in anger and frustration, when it's screamed in the dark from someone's crib, I know this is exactly the job I always wanted. My feet are finally still (maybe stuck to my dirty floor) and I'm not constantly looking for the exit. After a decade of pushing too much and trying too hard, I've finally come into my own, with none of the pomp and circumstance I always expected. As it turns out, mama is my best identity yet.

Six-Week Blowout

*I*t was the day of my six-week postpartum checkup; the day that men the world over rejoice and women dread. We were living several hours from family and all my friends worked, so I was forced to take Chase with me to the early morning appointment. I wasn't really sure what I'd do if he started losing it in the middle of the examination while I was naked from the waist down with someone's hand inside me, but I figured I'd cross that bridge when I got to it.

The beginning of the appointment went smoothly—Chase slept through the obnoxiously long waiting room stint and then promptly woke up as soon as we got into the exam room. I was still in that early stage of wanting to appear like I knew what the hell I was doing, so I pretended like I wasn't sweating through my clothes, as his fussing got increasingly louder with every second that passed. I bounced him in one arm while holding the starch-stiff sheet around my lower half, attempting to pay attention as the midwife tried to discuss birth control options over his screaming. Thankfully, the topic served to lighten the mood a little because, *seriously*? I had just stopped bleeding from childbirth like the day before and they actually expected me to pick out birth control? ("I'll take Abstinence for 1000, Alex.")

"I can have one of the nurses hold him for a few minutes while we do the exam," the midwife said charitably. "They love new babies." I felt bad handing my screaming infant off to a total stranger but I figured they were used to it and I could use the help. A youngish nurse came to collect him and off they went, with her smiling and cooing and him angrily wailing back. "We can make this quick," the midwife said before snapping on a pair of surgical gloves and pulling out the stirrups. I laid back on the examination table and let the midwife do her thing. She oohed and aahed and said it looked like I'd never given birth at all ("I bet you say that to all the girls," I teased) and then there was a knock at the door.

"He had a little accident," said the nurse who'd been watching my son for approximately six minutes. "He might need to be changed."

To this day, after two children and countless gruesome diaper changes, that "little accident" is the worst blowout I've ever seen. It was EVERYWHERE: up his back, all over his legs, in cracks and crevices I didn't know he had. I was genuinely surprised the nurse hadn't been a casualty of the blast radius. It was the kind of blowout that you'd assume gave the term its name.

I felt paralyzed, completely unsure what to tackle first: my naked lower half or my howling, poop-covered newborn. I thought back to the last diaper I used and was suddenly very unsure whether the diaper bag had any actual diapers left in it. I pushed aside the thought, unwilling to consider the absurd possibility that I had brought a bag so full it barely zipped which might not contain the one item for which it was named. I am an extremely modest person and the fact that I was still naked was horrifying to me. But I didn't want to look like I was putting myself before my child, so I felt obligated to take care of him first.

"Let's just lay him down right here," the nurse said and plopped him on the paper-covered examination table where my naked body had just been. There I was in the middle of the room, bare ass naked with a screaming, poop-covered infant and two medical professionals who were, undoubtedly, watching my every move with roadside traffic accident curiosity. In short, I was an actual shit show.

"We'll give you some privacy," the midwife said, intentionally avoiding a glance at my still-uncovered lower half. But it was too late; I'd already lost all sense of modesty. I wanted to yell, "Don't leave me alone with this disgusting tiny person!" I didn't, however, because as I was quickly learning, that disgusting person was my responsibility, for better or for worse.

Finally without an audience, I got to work tackling the issue in front of me. Although he's my child and I had already had all manner of his bodily fluids wiped and squirted on me over the last six weeks, this was a whole different ballgame. I grabbed a pair of the surgical gloves before diving in. I shucked off his pants as he wriggled and kicked and placed them on the paper-covered table. The poop bled through the paper, but I didn't have time to care. I had to move onto the rest of his outfit. *Shit, was that the doorknob?* Bent over the table with my bare ass hanging out, I was on high alert; everything sounded like a person entering the room, about to discover my nakedness. When the door opened to the room next door, I nearly jumped out of my skin. Come to think of it, being in pretty much anyone else's skin would've been preferable at that moment.

Did you know that onesies have those envelope folds at the top so you can roll them down over the baby after a blowout? I didn't. I pulled the saturated onesie over Chase's tiny shoulders and head, leaving a trail of poop from his butt to his scalp. I had to pause there to laugh about this adorable outfit I thought the nurses and midwives—maybe even other moms in the waiting room—would fawn over. It was beyond saving and went directly into the trashcan, along with his socks. The best laid plans.

Now here's where I learned an interesting thing about blowouts: it's possible for the poop to go everywhere on a baby's body—ears, hair, between the toes and in the folds of his legs—but almost completely avoid the vessel designed to hold it. I opened the diaper expecting to find another gruesome scene only to discover the poop had escaped through the very top of the back, leaving only a small stain before wreaking its havoc elsewhere. His butt was totally, ironically, clean. Not for the first time over the past six weeks, I wondered what the hell I'd gotten myself into.

Now I had to face the music of the diaper bag: were there any diapers in there? I pawed through it wildly, desperately, sweating even more profusely now as I imagined a scenario in which I'd have to wrap my baby in what was left of the paper from the table and march out into the world. Then, mixed in with all the bottles of hand sanitizer I'd yet to crack open and pacifiers he wouldn't touch, was one beautifully unmarred newborn diaper.

There was also at least half a package of wipes, which was going to be cutting it close, but was better than the wet gauze pads I envisioned myself using if I'd forgotten those too. I cleaned Chase up the best I could using every single wipe in the package, then put him in the new diaper. Naturally, the only outfit I had in the diaper bag was a one-size sleeper that opened at the bottom—definitely not conducive to being strapped into a car-seat—but at least I had something for him to wear. I hiked up the gown to his hips, placed him in the carseat and secured the straps over his bare legs. And then, after balling up the poop-stained paper covering on the table and putting clothes back on my lower half, we marched out into the world, unnecessary birth control prescription in hand.

Just call me the poster child for abstinence.

A Fly on the Wall

A fly on the wall of my life might call me a selfish mother, and that fly might be right. It might accuse me of putting my own needs before that of my son or wonder why I still enjoy some of the same luxuries as childless women my age. Maybe it would be onto something.

If that fly peeked into my world, it might see me waking early to avoid being accompanied into the shower by a pair of insistent little hands tugging at my soapy legs or watch me sneaking out the door on a Saturday morning for a solo run, untethered to a 30 pound jogging stroller and a bag of contingency distractions. It would likely catch a glimpse of me contentedly eating breakfast at the kitchen table while my son plays alone in the next room or sending him off to build block towers with daddy so mommy can edit a blog post in peace. It would have seen me skipping out for a date night with Adam when our son was barely two weeks old, gulping down vodka tonics in a crowded restaurant and desperately trying not to bring him up for fear we'd never have a normal adult conversation again. It might cast blame if it witnessed my toddler whining at my feet while he waits for me to apply a hasty coat of mascara or finish blow-drying my hair before we leave for the grocery store.

Maybe it wouldn't make sense to that fly why the needs of my son have not wholly subsumed my own, why I still consider my identity as a woman to be separate and distinct from my role as a mother. It would be well within its rights to say that I don't possess the necessary selflessness, the complete devotion everyone knows is the earmark of a good mom. It might even be correct.

But, maybe, just maybe, I'd have a leg to stand on when that fly questioned my motives because I'd have some validity on my side.

On that fateful day when my husband and I decided to pull the goalie, and I metaphorically inked my name on the waiting list for motherhood, I don't remember signing away my rights and needs as a person. I didn't agree to a lifetime of mom jeans and bad jokes, to being perpetually out of touch with current events and pop culture, to having eternally unwashed hair, a lapsed gym membership and no idea when I last ate.

Although the majority of my showers are joint ventures and some days I eat my breakfast at 12:30 p.m. over the kitchen trash can, I still reserve the right to have needs. I respect that my son is a person too, but his needs are equal to, not always more important than, my own.

I'd reason with that fly that it's OK to put your own needs before that of your children's sometimes, especially if it means your personal hygiene gets a nudge in the right direction. I'd assert that being a good mom and a fulfilled woman don't have to be mutually exclusive, even in the age of mommy wars and

"I'm-better-than-you-are" parenting. I'd argue that, per-haps, a little independence is a good thing for anyone, even our children.

In the face of genuine skepticism from that fly, I'd argue that my son and I will both be better off because I had the courage to be a little bit selfish. And maybe, just maybe, I'd be right.

Revoking My Stay-at-Home Mom Card

I think it's fair to say all stay-at-home-moms hate the phrase, "What did you do all day?" Even broached innocently (which it is probably 98% of the time), we automatically take it as a hostile interrogation intended to expose us for the frauds we worry we are.

So when my husband asks it nearly every evening after he gets home from work, I find myself automatically switching into defensive mode. Suddenly the smallest details of a perfectly ordinary day are exaggerated for maximum effect.

"Well Chase had a huge blowout and he's been really cranky all day—his teeth are bothering him *again*—and he barely napped at all," I recap in a huffy rush. "Plus the checkout line at the grocery store took forever and he basically cried the whole time."

I hear myself saying these things and I realize that I'm glossing over all the other details that made up a wholly pleasant day—the giggles while we sang songs in front of the mirror, the walk we took by the beach with the wind blowing through his white-blonde hair, the two whole hours he napped and I got to write or finish the dishes or watch just one teeny episode of House of Cards (alright, maybe three).

I don't talk about those things because I worry. I worry that if my day doesn't seem hard enough or chaotic enough, I'm not doing it right. I worry that my husband (and maybe the rest of the working world, too) thinks I'm getting a free ride on the gravy train. I worry that someone is going to come and revoke my stay-at-home-mom card.

I know. When it's written down, staring me in the face in black and white, the notion seems ridiculously hyperbolic and just plain crazy. I'm fully aware that there are no stay-at-home-mom police waiting to slap on the cuffs and drag me away because my son is an agreeable child with an affinity for taking long naps.

Yet I constantly feel the need to prove myself. To my husband. To other moms who work. To my friends who don't yet have kids. Prove to them that my work is hard too, that I'm not just milking the system. I think the reason I crave that validation is because the truth is, *some days, being a stay-at-home-mom is really freakin' easy.* On those days, I feel guilty.

I picture my husband busting his ass at work, looking over boring, complicated diagrams (or whatever the hell an electrical engineer actually does), staying late to impress his new boss while his wife whines in his ear about getting poop on her shirt.

I envision my former colleagues who work all day and then have to pick up the kids at daycare, cook an edible meal, give baths and check homework while half their brain is still occupied by the proposal they have to give in the morning. I think about my friends whose whole world is conference calls and productivity meetings and expense account lunches, whose workdays are long and demanding and certainly no afternoon walk at the beach with a happy baby.

And then I remember what it's like to work at a real job. I remember that sometimes people bring cupcakes into work. And sometimes you kill an hour looking at dumb memes that Helen from Accounting emailed out to the whole office. Sometimes your boss lets you cut out a little early because it's Friday and he wants to go home, too.

I remember that when you work in an office you get sick days and vacation time and no one spreads feces on you. I remember that, at most jobs, the client doesn't wake you up in the middle of the night because his teeth hurt or he peed the bed. I remember that at a regular job, your work is just work, not the all-consuming, terribly important endeavor of being responsible for someone's whole existence.

Then I remember that, even on the easy days, I'm still at work, too. The perks are just different.

Flicker

There it is, clear as day: a big, fat plus sign on the pregnancy test. Eleven days late, not wanting to get my hopes up, but unable to wait any longer. It comes as such a shock: we had no luck trying in October and then made the decision to wait until the new year, when finances were better, after all the parties and the drinking, when our insurance plan was more conducive to starting a pregnancy. And yet...

I am ecstatic.

Then the plans start: buying a tiny stocking with the word "baby" stitched on the outside to place on the mantel next to ours; sharing the news with our families at Christmas; double strollers, side-by-side nurseries, a family of four by next Christmas.

We are over the moon.

Weeks pass, slowly ticking down to the day we get to share the excitement with our families. The passage of time is torturously unhurried, the anticipation nearly boiling over as we struggle to keep our secret. Packages come: a big brother shirt for Chase, a photo calendar for my mom on which we plan to circle the due date. It's all falling into place.

We are positively giddy.

Then, on a Saturday morning while I'm baking cookies with Chase, I feel a rush of warmth between my legs. I excuse myself and walk hurriedly to the bathroom. Red. Dizzying amounts of red.

I yell for my husband from the top of the stairs, "Call the doctor." We play phone tag, describe the symptoms.

"Tell her I've had a miscarriage before," I remind him, as if he's forgotten, as if either of us can think about anything else.

"The offices are closed," she says, "you'll have to wait until Monday for an ultrasound. Unless you want to try the emergency room."

He hangs up.

"Our insurance won't cover an ER visit," he says calmly. "It will cost us at least $3,000."

"How can you ask me to wait two whole days to find out if our baby is alive?" I scream at him, my anger misplaced.

"It's up to you," he says, and I know he means it. "We'll do whatever you need to do."

"I can tell where you stand," I say bitterly. "We'll just wait until Monday to find out our baby is already gone."

We trudge through two long days while mindless TV shows loop continuously in the background. We cry; I yell. The bleeding continues. I count off all the things we've lost, memories that will never be made, wonder if Chase will be our only. I mourn for the first Christmas magic he won't get, the excitement we can't fake as we open gifts and struggle to keep our voices high and light. The Christmas lights stay off, the house dark except for the flicker of the TV.

Two losses in as many years. We are absolutely devastated.

Monday finally comes. "I want to see you in my office," the doctor says. We pack up Chase and get in the car. In the passenger seat, I am steely-eyed and stoic; it feels like we're driving to a funeral.

At the hospital, the ultrasound tech instructs me to "lay back on the table with your knees up." She angles the screen away from me; I angle my face away from hers—I don't want to see the look on it when she confirms our fears in black and white.

She points the screen back to me. I brace myself, white-knuckle grip Adam's hand. "See that little flicker?" she asks. That's the baby's heartbeat. One sixty four, nice and strong."

I can't believe it. My eyes well up, full of the tears I've been unable to summon this morning. Adam squeezes my hand, Chase squirms in his arms. It's so improbable, I wonder if she made a mistake. But no, there it is, that little flicker, the best sight I've ever seen. The overwhelming relief gives way to immediate guilt. I gave up. I don't deserve this baby.

And yet...

"There is a four-centimeter bleed in your uterus," the doctor explains. "Some women have much bigger bleeds and go on to have perfectly healthy babies. Some miscarry. It's all a waiting game. I wish I could tell you something more definitive."

I smile, because that flicker is the only definitive thing I need to know today. Our baby is still alive. So there's always hope.

Christmas is all about believing in things you can't see. The fictitious: Santa Claus, reindeer, elves and the North Pole. The real: God, the baby Jesus, Bethlehem and the manger. It's about trusting when you have scarcely little proof, about choosing to believe despite the doubts in your mind. This Christmas, I choose to believe.

I believe that I will still get my side-by-side nurseries and double stroller, that we will be a family of four next Christmas. I believe I will get the chance to look down at my swollen belly in the summer heat, that Chase will get the chance to be a big brother. I believe that the bleed will get smaller, the baby will get bigger and everything will turn out just fine.

I believe because it's the only thing I can do.

For now, we will be happy. Not cautious, just optimistic. Because, when a real, live Christmas miracle lands on your lap, there is no room for doubt.

The Things Moms Carry

An adaptation of *The Things They Carried* by Tim O'Brien.

he things moms carry have very little to do with necessity.
We carry spare pacifiers in every crevice of our purses, shoes for feet that can't yet walk, contingency Goldfish for screaming toddlers in Target. We carry diaper bags and backpacks and messenger bags laden with games and toys and accessories for the off-chance that one of them will be exactly what our child needs at any given moment.

We carry breasts heavy with milk, a few extra pounds in our midsections, bags under tired eyes that haven't known peaceful sleep since the plus sign appeared on the pregnancy test.

We carry the belief that any snot-nosed punk who picks on our kid at the playground deserves the handful of sand that was thrown in his eye, even if he is only three feet tall.

We carry the bone-deep weariness that is derived from a state of constant vigilance, from hyperawareness, from cradling feverish children at 3:00 a.m. when the pediatrician can't be reached and the phone just rings and rings.

The things moms carry are determined to some extent by pure madness.

We carry two extra lovies in case both of the others happen to go on hiatus with the stray socks and Tupperware lids. We carry baby wipes in our purses long after our children are potty-trained; we carry tiny knit blankets and newborn onesies with which we can't bear to part.

We carry a running list in our minds at all times of exactly what we need to get out of the house successfully. Tap shoes, swim goggles, the crunchy granola bars (no, I said *NOT THE CHEWY ONES*), the orange sippy cup with the blue lid and the purple dinosaur sticker on the bottom.

We carry our sleeping children, limbs dangling, heads lolling in blessed inertia amidst an existence marked by constant movement. We carry the guilt that our lives are too fast, too packed, too stretched at the seams to appreciate what it means to be truly still.

We carry the crushing worry that our child could someday be the victim we sadly shake our heads at on the news: the bullied, the assaulted, the child trapped in the classroom with a shooter roaming the halls. We carry the paralyzing fear that the same child, the one who couldn't sleep without a nightlight until age 11 and planned funerals for dead bugs, might someday be that very bully, that very rapist, that very shooter who brings harm to someone else's child.

We carry a torch for great dads everywhere; the ones with bottles poking out of their pockets in the grocery store, the ones sitting in business meetings with pink painted fingernails, the ones who know the names of all the Disney princesses and teach their sons about what it really means to be a man (bodily functions aside). We carry a special place in our hearts for the men who can still make their wives feel sexy after three kids and a c-section scar, the ones who lie and say it doesn't feel any different down there (really, they swear).

The things moms carry vary by situation.

Elizabeth's mom carries every single container of store-brand mixed berry yogurt that the supermarket stocked today, because it's the only thing her picky toddler will eat since last Wednesday. Lucas' mom carries ten pounds of putrid hockey gear to the washing machine every afternoon; Ella's mom the 64 art projects she finds that her daughter made at daycare this week when she empties her cubby on Friday.

Alex's mom carries his beloved blankie in her purse where he can't see it, because he said he's too old to bring it to his first sleepover. She carries it because she knows there's a chance he might still need its comfort when his courage falters at the last minute. Or that she will when he marches bravely into the house without it.

We carry the burden of not being *enough,* for our children and our selves: of not being physically present enough or emotionally available enough, of not being a strict enough disciplinarian or a lax enough dreamer, of letting our children's hopes and fears and aspirations crowd out our own.

We carry the regrets of all we didn't see, do or accomplish before our children were born: the foreign oceans in which we never skinny-dipped, the salsa class we never took, the bed we didn't appreciate until we had to share it with three other bodies during a thunderstorm or after a particularly scary cartoon.

We carry the unease of wondering if our next child could possibly be as loved, as perfect as the others, if they will complete our family or make us question why we tried again. We carry the absolute conviction that they can be loved as much and are every bit as perfect, at the very moment they enter the world

We carry those babies within our bodies for nine months that seem like nine years, warring with the feelings of reverent awe and utter annoyance. We carry their weight, their heft, their substantiality, every rib-kicking, bladder-pressing, this-week-he's-the-size-of-a-cantaloupe ounce. We carry them despite all the unknowns, until we learn them through osmosis—"he doesn't like loud noises, feel him kicking?"

And then they're born and we send them off into the world carrying our very existence in the palms of their hands.

Days Like This

Today was one of those days. You know the kind: the ones where you can't get out of your own way, where you half expect someone to show up and pry your mom badge from your bumbling, inept fingers.

I'm not talking about a day plagued by catastrophic occurrences, but those everyday nuisances that pile into one big snowball of shit that seems to gather steam as the day rolls on. The days that sound ridiculous to complain about in comparison to world hunger and foreign wars but seem 100% justified in the heat of the moment with a screaming toddler whose favorite blanket was accidentally abandoned in aisle three of the grocery store (or was it Wal-Mart? or the bank?).

Today our shit storm hit at the doctor's office, or more precisely, on the way out the door to the doctor's office. I had arranged childcare for Chase in advance so I could go by myself, but it fell through and I found myself already out of the house and without a stroller to keep him contained during the appointment.

I remember well my last doctor's appointment. I watched him with one eye during my pap smear while he crawled around the not-really-all-that-clean-for-a-doctor's-office floor. Not wanting to repeat that, I stopped for an umbrella stroller (which I'd been meaning to buy anyway) to lessen the inconvenience of having Chase with me.

We searched the drugstore and, miracle of miracles, they actually had one left. Twenty bucks later we marched out to the parking lot, ready for the doctor's office. Little did I know that every single part of the damn thing was fused together with zipties, so when we pulled up to the office with only a few minutes to spare I had no way of getting it to open. (Picture me in the trunk of my Jeep, straddling the stroller and attempting to use one of my keys to saw the pieces off like an extremely un-resourceful version of Tom Hanks in *Castaway*). Having given up, I went inside to the appointment carrying Chase in one arm and the stroller in the other, the irony not lost on me. At the front desk, I stood reciting my phone number, street address and birthdate to the receptionist while struggling under the weight of a 25-pound toddler, 30-pound diaper bag and totally useless still-zip-tied umbrella stroller.

I asked for scissors and the receptionist was kind enough not to gawk openly as I fumbled with the plastic ties that held the Fort Knox stroller together. Meanwhile my child was crawling around the dirty carpet where I unceremoniously dumped him, now unexplainably sockless and with his hat covering his eyes. I was actually sweating through my shirt trying to attach the wheels to the stroller (why were they not already attached, dammit?!), keenly aware of every eye in the waiting room on the spectacle that was me: unprepared and bumbling, with a very visible baby bump and a child under a year that I frantically stuffed into the stroller while the nurse waited impatiently at the door.

We were shuffled into the bathroom to give a urine sample where I accidentally peed on my hand, which stung like crazy because of the thousands of tiny little cracks on my skin from which my unborn child was constantly siphoning moisture and nutrients. I didn't bother to wipe off the container because I reasoned that the person on the other side was probably wearing gloves and having a better day overall than I was.

We met with a new doctor who said by way of introduction, "Do you feel like you were *just* pregnant? Probably because you were, you crazy lady!" Normally this might be cause for a laugh, but instead it just served to infuriate me as she patted me on the back like I was ripe for picking at the insane asylum. The rational part of me knew she was just trying to be funny. The hormonal part of me kind of wanted to stab her with the Mirena pen I could've easily nabbed from her front pocket.

In the span of five minutes, she decried my choice of footwear for the weather (Converse sneakers, which she deemed "so cute, but not very warm or safe") remarked again on the fact that I seemed to be pregnant after *just* having a baby and told me that I lost five pounds since I last came to the doctor's office a month ago. I felt like I was back in my nutritionist's office at the outpatient eating disorders clinic, getting my wrist slapped for not maintaining my weight.

"Are you eating enough?" she asked in what was probably a very nonjudgmental tone but to me felt like an insult. I assured her I was and that I've been consuming enough ice cream sundaes to feed a small African village. All at once, I was so very done with the conversation, the appointment, the day.

As we exited the exam room, I felt defeated and inept. It often seems like the times when I struggle the most as a mother are the ones when I have an audience. Though the witnesses to my mistakes and missteps probably aren't judging me the way I assume they are, the weight of my shortcomings feels that much heavier when there are spectators present. I often wonder if the nurse at our pediatrician's office thinks I'm perpetually unprepared since I never remember to bring Chase's shot records or if the librarian who's witnessed him pushing the elevator alarm more than once believes I can't control my child. Maybe both of those assessments are accurate.

I know this was one of those "mountain out of a molehill" situations. Nothing all that terrible happened; it just *felt* terrible in the moment, as those little details of motherhood sometimes do. Days like this will come along every now and then—sometimes more in any given week than the good days, if I'm being realistic. But there's always tomorrow, and if that day goes to shit too, at least I've already got the damn stroller assembled.

Waiting for the Other Shoe

I've never considered myself to be a pessimist, my glass is often half full and I typically don't get caught up in worrying about things I can't control. Overall, I'm a pretty happy person whose company enough people enjoy. That being said, I've had a terrible, lifelong habit of perpetually waiting for the other shoe to drop, of fearing that all the bad, ugly, painful things in life will, at some point or another, balance the good.

I honestly don't know from where or what this apprehension stems, but I carry it buried deep under my skin, like a rabbit's foot with a contrary purpose, a talisman for bad luck. It is the weight of a thousand unspoken worries and feverish, winged prayers, it is the unquiet in my mind that whispers, "Life is too good. Happiness is never free, you know."

I get it. That makes me sound like some crazy naysayer who believes no one can truly be content in his or her own happiness. And 98% of the time I don't feel that way at all. I enjoy the hell out of my life and I try to live in the moment as much as possible, to see the world through the eyes of my son, who is just as fascinated by the speck of lint on the carpet as the entire playroom awash in primary colors and toys just for him.

But that 2%—the part that I am constantly stuffing down and drowning out—that part worries how I will pay for my current happiness: a cancer diagnosis, the death of a loved one, a fracture in my beautiful marriage. And, now that I am a mother, there's just so much more to lose. It absolutely terrifies me.

After my first pregnancy ended in a miscarriage, I vividly remember telling Adam how scared I was that it would ruin all subsequent pregnancies for me, that I'd never be able to relax in the knowledge that our future unborn children were OK. But then a crazy thing happened when I got pregnant again: *I felt completely calm.* I knew right away that this baby was going to be fine. I felt like I'd paid my penance and weathered so much unimaginable suffering the first time, that this pregnancy would be entirely immune to problems.

And, for all intents and purposes, it was. I skated by with minimal morning sickness, gained enough but not too much weight and, when it came time for our son's birth, labored for only six hours with 20 minutes of pushing. Our baby was healthy, I had survived his birth and Adam and I were deliriously happy. Life couldn't be better.

But then, the doubts started to creep in. Did an easy pregnancy mean that I'd have to pay in some other way? Would my son be a colicky, purple-faced wailer, up all hours of the night? Would he be delayed somehow, lagging behind other children his age? Would he be endlessly unhappy or inconsolable, one of those babies that other parents are so glad they didn't end up with?

But it soon became very clear that our champion sleeper who is almost never without a smile and some crusty peanut butter on his face, was none of those things. He is as close to perfect as I can imagine. And, day-by-day, I'm learning to not let that scare the everloving shit out of me.

Now that I'm pregnant with my second, I wonder, at times, if I'm paying for my firstborn's easygoing nature and affinity for sleeping 12 hours a night. This pregnancy has been fraught with problems and complications and I can't help but feel it's a result of something more than pure circumstance, though I'm very aware that's not how it works.

I know, deep down in my bones, that happiness does not beget sadness, pleasure does not precipitate pain. There's not some register that tallies our every good and bad experience, and a tick mark in the "good" column, doesn't have to be balanced by one in the "bad." I understand that expecting hard times doesn't make you more prepared to deal with them, it only robs you of your happiness when things are good. And I know there will be bad times; it's just part of the business of being alive. But I've had plenty of those before and, I'm still here, weathering the rough days with as much grace as I can muster.

All of that makes sense when I write it out on paper and I really do believe it. But the vigilant watch for that other shoe is the habit of a lifetime that's hard to break.

Thankfully, being a mother has also taught me to appreciate the small things, the stuff that we adults gloss over in our constant hurry to get where we think we need to go. Little by little, my son is teaching me to push my worries aside for more immediate concerns, to let the reality and tangibility of the now take up more headspace than the fuzzy unknown of the future.

He is my perpetual reminder of what it actually means to live in the present moment, to focus singularly on only that which is directly in front of you.

Even if what's directly in front of you is nothing more than a particularly fascinating piece of carpet lint.

The Worry of Two

"**A**re you sure you're ready to do this all over again?" my husband asks abruptly, turning to me in bed.

I pause, resting my spoon in the bowl of Breyer's cookie dough ice cream balanced on my 8-month-pregnant belly. "Nope. Not even close. You?"

"No, but I think it's a little too late for that," he says, gesturing to my swollen midsection where our cabbage-sized baby is currently starting his nightly aerobics.

It is a familiar conversation, one we'd had when our first baby swam inside me, both of us a tangle of nerves as the full weight of the unknown settled over us each night. Fifteen months later, about to do it all again, I feel that familiar anxiety rise up in my gut and I am prepared to stuff it down like I have so many times over the last 32 weeks.

But tonight I decide instead to let it sit, allowing myself to truly feel the entire spectrum of worry I've glossed over in favor of other, less-terrifying distractions. Like the heaping basket of laundry in the corner or the half-finished tile installation that has caused a bathroom vanity, washer and dryer to take up residence in our small bedroom for several weeks. Those other concerns have been on my mind all day, but I am not giving them any more credence tonight. My child is coming in two short months and I owe him five minutes of an undistracted mind before I slip into fitful sleep.

The worry of two. In the quiet darkness, this unease terrifies me more than any nightmare my pregnant brain can conjure up.

I watch myself chasing after a spirited toddler with a baby clamped to my breast, desperately trying to get him to latch so he'll cease his purple-faced screaming. I see myself torn between meeting two equally-urgent demands, without the ability to satisfy both. I feel weight of guilt permanently sagging my shoulders like dense chainmail, trying to explain to my older but still-very-young son why mommy can't play with him right this minute.

I picture those side-by-side nurseries I dreamt of so many months ago coming back to haunt me, the thin walls the only barrier between my wailing infant and my light-sleeping toddler. When they wake at the same time, how will I know which one to comfort first? Is it the one whose needs are most urgent or do I keep a running tally so I know who was slighted last time?

I see my soft, fleshy postpartum body on display in a summer tank top instead of the sweatshirts I hid under the first time, with no hours in the day and nowhere near enough energy to transform it back to its pre-baby shape. I see repeated attempts at going to the gym undermined by mismatched naptimes and errands that will not run themselves. I picture the double jogging stroller sitting untouched in the basement because, despite the grand plans I had when it was purchased, I'm not sure I will ever have enough motivation to actually use it.

I envision the lonely, tear-filled days stretched out like a flat country interstate, with only brief respite from the monotony during the short hours my husband takes the wheel. I remember how easy it was for me to slip into depression once. I worry that it will be even easier this time.

I see my bumbling inadequacy spotlighted in a grocery store as I try to manage two children so close in age that I have trouble handling them both by myself. I might begin to believe that the naysayers must have been right when they told me I was crazy to get pregnant again so soon.

The worry of two is almost paralyzing when I give it my full attention, which is why I so rarely do. I know there is no preparing for it, no amount of *you'll be fine*'s and *try not to worry*'s that will ease my disquieted mind.

Part of me wants to believe that by embracing the coming struggle, leaning into the full-force gales that are about to mix up the dust, I will be less surprised when the storm hits. Instead of barricading myself in my basement while I wait for the inevitable, I will stand boldly on the front lawn and watch the clouds roll in, hoping my awareness will make it easier to weather.

I know it's not all doom and gloom. Having a second child will multiply more than just our exhaustion and worry; it will amplify our capacity for love, deepen our pool of happiness, stretch and grow our little family until it feels like we've always been a foursome. So much good will come from adding a second child to our lives. Yet I also feel compelled to expect a less-than-seamless transition, in case that little bit of readiness helps prepare me for that which I cannot possibly ever be fully prepared.

So my answer is still *no, I'm not ready*. But maybe accepting that is half the battle.

Originally published on Mamalode.com

Kind of Woman

When I was younger, I thought I'd be the kind of woman who remembers people's birthdays off the top of her head.

Without a doubt, I'd be the kind who sends anniversary cards that arrive on the exact date, who mails thank-you notes in an appropriate amount of time and pens "just thinking of you" letters on pretty stationery for no reason at all. I didn't foresee becoming the kind of woman whose thank-you arrives four months too late and stretches wedding gift giving to the upper limit of the customary one-year mark.

I thought I'd be the kind of woman who makes her children chocolate chip pancakes for breakfast and tucks notes into lunchboxes stuffed with balanced, nutritionally-sound meals. I didn't envision myself buying overpriced yogurt tubes and calling them a meal or letting ketchup become a major food group in our household.

I thought I'd be the kind of woman with easy, flawless pregnancies, who loved every minute of gestation and couldn't wait to fill her house with four—maybe five—babies so we could be just like the chaotic but tight-knit sitcom families of my youth. I had no idea I'd lose my very first pregnancy then wish away my pregnant body in exchange for a glass of red wine, or that I would consider stopping at two children because they're much more expensive than I realized.

I thought I'd be the kind of woman whose house is clean more often than not, who folds clothes each night, whose feet don't turn black when she walks barefoot on her kitchen floor. I am sincerely surprised that I still haven't somehow morphed into my own mother, whose house is always spick and span when compared with my cluttered hoarder house.

I thought I'd be the kind of woman who would always be at home in her own skin, who wouldn't pinch and scrutinize and cover up from shame or discomfort. I certainly didn't expect to be the kind of woman who throws away most of her early 20s clawing through a debilitating eating disorder that robbed her of every last shred of self-love and would take nearly a decade from which to recover.

I had grand visions in my head of the woman I would someday become. These images stayed with me as I navigated my late teens and early 20s; I figured I still had plenty of time to make them a reality. Once I entered my mid 20s, I saw the mantle of adulthood being handed down from my parents. I was now the head of my own household—it was time I started bringing thoughtful gifts to family parties instead of tacking my name onto the bottom of my parents' cards and letting their buffalo chicken dip serve as a contribution from all of us.

I was in my late 20s with one baby and another on the way when it finally dawned on me: *maybe this is who I was meant to be.*

These days I'm much happier, having finally given up the ghost of that woman who haunted me for most of my adult life. I can accept that I have many good qualities, even if sending timely thank you cards and remembering to dust my fan blades are not among them.

For the first time in my life I am happy with the kind of woman I am, even if she's a far cry from the kind of woman I thought I'd eventually become. Maybe I never had it in me to be the organic-lunch-packing, just-thinking-of-you-card-sending, pregnant-body-loving woman I always saw myself becoming someday. Maybe I needed to finally let go of the kind of woman I thought I'd be to truly love and respect the woman I really am.

When You Don't Know If It's the Last Pregnancy

The end of my first pregnancy couldn't come fast enough. I was uncomfortable, weary and anxious to meet the little person who tumbled and kicked his way through nine slow months inside me. Whenever people asked how much longer I had left, I automatically rounded up. Seventeen weeks was presented as "almost halfway;" six weeks until my due date became five or, depending how eager I was in that moment, "just over a month." I was in a rush to breeze through the race in anticipation of the gold medal waiting at the finish line.

Now, with only a matter of weeks left in my second pregnancy, I find myself holding tight to this moment, wishing time would slow down rather than speed up. Not because I'm more comfortable, have more energy or feel less anxious to meet my second baby. It's because I have no idea if this is the last time I will carry a child inside me.

It's a strange feeling, the not knowing. If you'd told me several years ago that I might be done having children by 28, I'd have laughed in your face and explained that you were sorely mistaken. If you'd said that I'd only have two kids, just 17 short months between them, I'd have told you all about the three or four we planned to add to our family, each appropriately spaced at least two years apart.

Two and done was never the plan, but neither was the crushing miscarriage of my first pregnancy. Or the inability to produce enough milk to feed my firstborn. Or the uterine bleed that lasted most of the first and second trimesters of my current pregnancy and had me so consumed with worry and anxiety that I suddenly stop seeing a third baby as a foregone conclusion.

Several months ago, as I lay stretched out on the examination table waiting for the results of the ultrasound to tell me whether or not those dark spots near my baby's brain were cysts like the doctors thought them to be, I was convinced this was it. "This will be our last baby," I thought, without a trace of doubt. "I couldn't take this again." *I clutched my swollen belly and I just knew.*

As those days and weeks and months of tear-filled anxiety recede in the rearview, I hear myself starting to talk about a third baby again. "I'd need years to recover from this pregnancy," I tell my husband, "but maybe I could do it if I had enough time to forget."

Then the other unknowns rear their ugly heads, endless white noise filling up my restless brain.

Right now, there will be one child for each of us. We are not yet outnumbered. That means mommy can take the oldest to Saturday morning swim class while daddy brings the youngest to karate. It means we can split up at the water park so the boy under 36 inches can play in the splash park while the taller one accompanies daddy on the fast slide. There are enough rooms in our house, there is enough space in our modestly sized cars. Right now, there is enough of everything to go around, but with three? Maybe not.

Money is tight enough with one baby, let alone two, or—someday—three. Would it be irresponsible to bring a third child into our lives if it meant less of everything for each of them? Or would we be so happy to add another child to our family that we wouldn't miss the family vacations we can't afford to take, the extra items on the grocery list that aren't in the budget this week, the summer camps and sports teams we just can't make work this time around?

Adam grew up with next to nothing but has a childhood full of memories that revolve around his two brothers. I grew up solidly middle class—rarely wanting for anything— with only one sister with whom to share my parents' love, attention and finances, yet I longed for more siblings. I craved the chaos of a life like the one from my husband's childhood. What will my children want? What will we want? I clutch my swollen belly and I just don't know.

I realize how preemptive this line of thought seems—I am not even finished gestating my second baby and already thinking about whether or not there will be a third—but a small part of me worries that I will have wasted the end of my last pregnancy complaining about lower back pain or glossing over those oh-so-often rib kicks that I may never feel again. What if this is it and I'm not savoring every last second?

I am a believer in God and I know His plan trumps mine; He is probably up there laughing at my incessant wondering and worrying because my life's plot has already been written, without need of my input. But I'm a planner, too, a thinker and a grand-schemer, and something about the unknown of a might-be-the-last-but-not-quite-sure pregnancy is unsettling.

The many mothers who have come before me say you just know when your family is complete, and I firmly believe I will, whether that's in 30-something days when our second son is born or many years from now when we welcome a third to our family. At this moment, it's all coming up question marks. For now, I will regard my swollen belly with reverence and count the kicks with awe, just in case it's the last time. Because maybe I'm just not meant to know.

You Won't Remember, But I Will

"**H**e'll never remember life before his brother," everyone tells me when I let the guilt of ending your time as an only child seep in. "To him, it'll always have been this way."

I know they're right, and their assurances give me comfort in those quiet moments when I feel a rush of remorse stronger than the swell of a tidal wave that threatens to demolish everything in its path. The fact that you won't remember our time before your brother—a time I have cherished more than you can ever imagine—is often even harder to come to grips with than the fact that this era is coming to an end.

But I know it's true: you won't remember.

You won't remember the early days when we learned how to be a twosome; that first day when daddy's car disappeared around the corner, off to work and another life while I sobbed holding you, tiny and new, wondering how I'd ever survive taking care of you alone for nine unrelentingly lonely hours.

You won't remember that we found our groove, you and I; that we built a life and a routine all our own, filling our days with stroller walks and picnics in the park, aquarium outings and play dates with new friends. You won't remember the lazy days when we never left the house, when we ate pancakes for breakfast and snuggled up on the couch watching Curious George in our pajamas well into the early afternoon.

You won't remember how doted-upon and spoiled you were; mommy and daddy's first baby, Nani and Grandpa's first grandchild, the first to smile and crawl and walk as we cheered you on like maniacs and filled up our memory cards with 8 billion pictures of your towheaded, gummy-smiled self. You won't remember that all the clothes and books and toys were yours first and that, for 17 months, you never had to share them with anyone at all.

You won't remember that you were the first to make me a mother, to give me the most fulfilling, life-affirming job on the planet. You won't remember that you literally changed my entire world the very moment that you entered it, red-faced and wrinkly, gulping lungfuls of new air; that the second the nurse placed you on my chest, I loved you with a ferocity I could have never comprehended in a thousand previous lives before you.

Thankfully, you also won't remember the steep learning curve of new motherhood and all the times I royally screwed it up. Like the time I didn't pack an extra outfit in your bag and you had to ride home from the store in just a diaper with snow still blanketing the ground outside. Or the time daddy had to run to Wal-Mart during our first real outing with friends because I somehow left only the nipple to your bottle at home. Or all the many times I failed you in little ways—losing my patience, letting you watch too much TV, prioritizing the wrong things over my precious time with you—ways that your lack of early memory will whitewash over, never to be remembered. In some ways, this is a silver lining—you will naturally forgive me all the mistakes you can't recall—but in others, it's heartbreaking. For every little thing I'm grateful you'll forget, there are at least a hundred more I wish so desperately you could remember.

No, you won't remember those first months and I know it's just as well. You will grow up to know nothing of life before your brother, that slightly smaller boy who tags along beside you, stealing away the toys you don't remember were once solely yours. You will never remember that you once had mommy and daddy all to yourself, that our attention was never split or compromised, which thankfully, will protect you from jealousy over your brother's arrival. It's true that there was a method to our madness when we mapped out our family plan and chose to have you both so close together, even though my guilt sometimes keeps me from remembering that.

You won't remember any of it before now. It's a clean slate, a new beginning as a family of four.

But that's why I'm here: because I will. I'll remember it all—every precious second. I'll remember for us both.

A New Life

The day we came home from the hospital with my younger son, Sam, was one of the most emotionally charged days of my life. To be fair, I was on a hormonal rollercoaster, giddy one minute and sobbing like a lunatic the next, so I'm sure our homecoming only added fuel to the fire. Our older son, Chase, had stayed at our house with my parents for the two days we were in the hospital and when we pulled into the driveway he was outside scooting across the pavement on a new ride-on toy my mom had bought him while we were gone. In the past, he'd spent plenty of overnights at both sets of grandparents' houses and it wasn't the first time we'd been gone for two whole days. But it was the first time we'd left him to give our undivided attention to the newest member of our family and it felt like the beginning of many future slights he'd have to endure.

At only 17 months, Chase was still my little boy, just a baby himself. In recent weeks, when I'd refer to him as my baby, Adam was quick to correct me: "He's not going to be the baby anymore," he reminded me. He'd always be my baby, I told Adam, even when he was 35 years old with babies of his own. Right then he was still so new to the world himself and the only existence he'd known up until this point was about to change literally overnight. In that instant, watching him from the car window just moments before we shook up the snow globe of our lives, the weight of the decision to add to our family so quickly came crashing down on me. It felt like the death of something, the end of our precious family of three. It was the birth of something beautiful, to be sure, but also an overpowering loss that made my eyes fill and the center of my chest ache.

Many people had given me advice about how to handle the initial encounters between Chase and the baby, so I was prepared to expect anything. While we were in the hospital, Chase had come to visit us twice with my parents, but this was the first time he'd realize that the tiny person he'd met on those occasions had come home with mommy and daddy. It made me ache for him, thinking of how young he was to be processing this change without any real understanding of what it all meant. I'd always thought having them close together would help make the transition smoother because Chase would have very little frame of reference for what was 'normal' in his world, but that day I realized how desperately I wanted him to be able to understand. I told him that mommy and daddy loved him and weren't replacing him, but that this baby, his little brother, was here to stay.

I carried Sam into the house in his car seat while Adam followed behind with Chase. We hugged him and told him how much we'd missed him; we made enthusiastic noises when he paraded in front of us, showing off each of his new toys from my parents and other well-wishers. In the kitchen, Sam dozed in the car seat, oblivious to anything happening around him. I knew enough not to force Chase to interact with the baby if he wasn't ready, so we let him play, watch TV, eat some of the food our friends and family had brought to the house. And then, ever so slowly, he moved in the direction of the car seat, still sitting unceremoniously in the middle of the kitchen floor. He peeked over the edge and studied Sam for a minute, sizing him up. He touched the tiny hospital bracelets on Sam's legs, rubbed the top of his head like a good luck talisman. Hope bubbled inside my chest, but it didn't erase the aching feeling I'd carried around all evening. And then, just like it had always been that way, he gave him a kiss before darting off again.

That night I was a wreck. The hormones had gotten the best of me and I had to retreat to the bathroom to sob quietly while Adam helped Chase get ready for bed. After pulling myself together, I entered Chase's room where they were reading books on the floor and handed the baby off to Adam. "I need to be the one who rocks him to sleep tonight," I said and I knew he understood.

Chase and I settled into the rocking chair and, as always, he draped his chubby legs around my midsection and settled his sweaty head into the curve of my neck. More often than not he won't tolerate being rocked to sleep. He might allow a song or maybe two if he's especially tired, but he's usually in a hurry to climb into his crib and snuggle up with his blankets and stuffed animals, ever the independent soul. My mom had said the only occasion when he'd shown signs of really missing us was during bedtime, and that night he let me rock him until I ran out of songs to sing and had to start over again. The lullabies I sang were interrupted more than once by violent sobs as tears leaked from my eyes and slid down my cheeks and into his mop of blonde hair.

I was, undoubtedly, in love with our new baby, but the regret in my heart was profound and overwhelming; I'd made an unfathomable mistake and I didn't know how to fix it. So I stayed in that chair and hugged him fiercely, inhaling his sweet little boy scent while the tears continued to slide down my cheeks and the sobs wracked my aching chest. As long as I stayed in that chair, holding him close, I could pretend nothing had changed; I could ignore my grief and guilt and regret and just be there in that moment with the little boy who had taught me how to be a mother. So that's exactly what I did. Until it was time to place him in his crib, back slowly out of the room and face the new life on the other side of the door.

Before You Walked Through the Door

Before you walked through the door, I was already gone. Grand visions of catching a Greyhound and heading for the border danced in my head as I chiseled day-old oatmeal off the tile and shouted, "Stop climbing that!" for the 43rd time in an hour. Before you even got to your parking spot, I was clocked out, off duty, my out-of-office message ready to ping back the next person who urgently needed my attention. In my mind, I'd already deposited the kids into your open arms as I made off toward my running sneakers or a bottle opener—whichever made the strongest bid for my interest.

Before you walked through the door, I wanted, for once, not to need you so desperately. I wanted to be the type of wife that doesn't get impatient when her husband says his meeting ran late or asks if he can stop off for a quick haircut before coming home. I want to encourage you to have beers with the guys from work or go to the gym for the first time in eight months, to do something for yourself that you never get to do because my dire need to be relieved of parent duty always unfairly trumps whatever it is that you need.

Before you walked through the door, I was ready to fill your ear with thoughts about how hard being a stay at home mother is. I wanted you to know that the baby spit up in my hair and the toddler helped himself to a sip of a stranger's iced coffee at the playground, and that no one napped and that's why dinner is cold cereal instead of the Creamy Chicken Pasta that's penciled in for Wednesday on the chalkboard. I wanted you to respect and admire me for all I do for our family and assure me that even your demanding 9 to 5 job is not nearly as challenging as raising two young children.

Before you walked through the door, I wanted you to be proud of how well I'm managing at home. I rushed to hastily clean up the house that I'd neglected all day—wiping down counters, herding stray toys into bins and baskets, stacking unwashed dishes neatly in the sink so it appears like it's only one load instead of two. I wanted you to see that, today, I'm keeping my head above water, even if I'm all but sinking from the shoulders down.

Before you walked through the door, I wished I had time to look nice for you. I wanted to be desirable and put together—some color in my cheeks and shine to my lips—the way the old me was before I stopped being me and started being only someone's mother. At the very least, when you walked through the door, I wanted to be wearing real pants.

And then you finally walk through the door, a collared shirt-and khaki-clad superhero, and you are the answer to all my exhaustive prayers of the last half hour. You apologize for running behind and compliment how good dinner smells, ask how you can help now that you're here (no, you don't mind chopping the peppers while holding the baby and taking out the trash at the same time). You tell me I smell nice, though surely that's a lie, and pour me a glass of Cab with one hand while juggling a kid who's screaming about the Goldfish he was slighted in the other. Even though five minutes ago I wanted not to need you so desperately, I undeniably do and I doubt that will change whether our children are toddlers or teenagers or have children of their own. Sure, we do alright when you're not here—there are play dates and library trips and swim classes that fill up our days—and I know how lucky I am to be the one on this side of the door all day. But if it's all the same to you, I'll always prefer the moment after you walk through the door to all the ones before it.

Cherish This Time

Every so often when I'm in a public place with my children, I become keenly aware of another person's stare nearly burning a hole through me. I'll be toting Sam around in the front pack while asking Chase to put back (insert item he's taken off the shelf here) and responding to his outside-voice-volume chatter when suddenly I experience that feeling you get when you're certain that someone is looking at you.

I'm never quite sure of the reason for strangers' looks: sometimes it's general appreciation for the cuteness of young children and sometimes it's curiosity at the fact that I seem to have two kids very close in age. Almost always, the person is quite a bit older. They catch my eyes as we pass in the aisle or wait in line at the bank and smile genuinely at me, taking in the full effect of the harried mom with two kids who is just barely maintaining composure as her toddler sprints away for the tenth time. More often than not the look they give is one of intense longing, an ache so palpable it's like a separate entity from the person feeling it.

They see me and the strangest thing happens: it's like I'm watching them as they catapult back in time to when they were here, in my shoes, a young mom or dad to a brood of rowdy children. Time has a way of spackling over the hard parts and smoothing the rough edges, leaving their perspective beautifully unmarred, offering up perfectly intact memories of the days when their children were still this little. "Cherish this time," they implore me and the words are desperate, solemn; sometimes it includes a hand on my arm or a conspiratorial smile. "It goes by too fast."

"I'm trying," I tell them, and that's the truth. I am trying. Not always succeeding, but trying at the very least.

Sometimes when I'm in the middle of a particularly beautiful moment with my children, I get this peculiar feeling of watching it all from a distance, as if my life were a movie and this exact moment is one that would surely wind up in the trailer. My husband will be tickling Chase until he coaxes that gorgeous, infectious laugh from his mouth and makes his eyes squint in pure enjoyment and I think, *Pay attention, Melissa. This is it. This is one of those moments that people talk about missing when their children are grown.* It's an undeniably odd experience. Most of the time I can appreciate the beauty of the moment and let that be enough. At other times it produces an ache in my chest that, although I am a writer by trade, I don't think I could ever accurately describe. It is longing and regret, desperation and mourning all captured in that painful knot behind my breast. I know the moment will not last forever; it is as tenuous and fragile as a soap bubble, ready to pop without warning and vanish into thin air. In moments like that, the sobering reality of my boys' childhood disappearing so quickly is enough to make me want to clutch them tight to me and never let go.

Then there are those other moments, the ones that the older parents in the grocery aisle have largely forgotten because they've been crowded out of their minds by nostalgic replacements. They are the moments when I'm awake in the middle of the night, stripping sheets off a bed covered in someone else's bodily fluids. They are the times when I'm desperate for Chase's touch only to have him deny me yet again and it feels like a knife directly through the center of my chest. They're the phases I don't particularly care for, the seasons of our lives that I find myself wishing away, and then feel guilty for not cherishing all of it and discriminating against harder moments in favor of good ones. Just the other day, Chase hit his brother over the head with the remote, causing pained shrieking from one and a timeout for the other. As Adam carted Chase off to timeout, I said, "I will be very happy when he's through this phase," and then immediately wanted to suck the words back into my mouth. Shouldn't I be cherishing all of it? Even the not-so-great parts? Is there a how-to guide for all this cherishing business?

To me, cherishing is an art form, one that must be studied and perfected over time. It has to be the right balance of appreciation for the moment and awareness of how quickly it will pass. It can't weigh too heavily in favor of one or the other because all you'd do is either breeze through your children's lives without noticing time passing or waste the gift of their childhood mourning the fact that it will all come to an end someday.

Whoever truly has it figured out must have a method I haven't quite perfected myself yet. I want to ask those people how they do it. I want to know how to fully cherish the little moments of my children's lives and still get laundry folded and dinner on the table before 8:00 p.m.. I want to understand how to appreciate the hard moments and not get weighed down by the heartbreaking impermanence of the good moments. I want to learn this art form now—while they're still young—before I become the woman in the store full of nostalgic regret, staring longingly at the young mother who is still in the thick of things. I don't want to waste little moments because I didn't realize they were actually the big ones.

Lately, those cautionary urgings pop into my head during the moments when things feel particularly hard. They are often the reminder I need that all of it is fleeting and none of it is worth getting too worked up over. When I'm dragging Chase by the arm through the store because he's suddenly refused to budge from the middle of Aisle 6, I grit my teeth, bite back an angry admonishment and try to remember how impermanent it all is—the good and the bad. When I'm up for the third time in as many hours during the middle of night with Sam, I picture him grown and gone, no longer needing me and I try like hell to keep his incessant need of that moment from breaking me. I'm not always successful in my endeavor to cherish our time together. The tantrums and spills and sleepless nights and messy everything is sometimes more than enough to make me forget about cherishing altogether.

But I am trying. Not always succeeding, but trying all the same.

Mail-It-In Mom

On Mondays, I'm a mail-it-in mom.

Where Sunday was once a day of rest, it is now a day of birthday parties and errands, car trips and family outings from which to recover.

On Mondays, there are no aquarium trips or music classes, because on Mondays, leaving the house is rare.

On Mondays, Curious George and Handy Manny are welcome visitors in our living room.

On Mondays, breakfast might be a hotdog bun smeared with peanut butter and lunch is likely to be cobbled together with stale crackers and various condiments from the fridge. Grey Poupon and Smuckers on Ritz anyone?

On Mondays, clean clothes are hard to come by and pants are optional.

On Mondays, I cling to Adam like a barnacle when he departs for work, begging him to take a sick day. On no Monday has this ever actually worked in my favor.

On Mondays, cleaning up from the Sunday night tornado seems like a much better idea than it did when it was actually Sunday night and a Netflix binge-session was just a click away.

On Mondays, chocolate consumption starts before 9:00 a.m. and the cork pops before 5:00 p.m.

On Mondays, everything seems just a little bit harder and just a little bit slower.

Mondays are for pajamas until noon and not worrying about the sorry state of the pantry. They're for eating foraged snacks on the sofa and watching the world pass us by out the window of the house we don't leave. Mondays are just what we need to recharge our batteries and make it to Tuesday in one piece.

On Tuesdays, there might be swim classes and doctors appointments and story books and play dates. But on Mondays, we mail it in. And we feel OK about it.

Unless, of course, it's raining on Tuesday. In which case there's always Wednesday.

I Still Don't Love My Postpartum Body

ive weeks postpartum, I stood naked in the front of the bathroom mirror feeling like I was staring at a stranger. I assessed my reflection honestly—not with hatred but with genuine wonderment. Some of the features were recognizable—the deep brown eyes, the slight gap between the front two teeth, the small circular birthmark on the collarbone—but that was where the familiarities ended. Nearly everything else had changed in some way throughout the past nine months, as my body morphed and swelled to accommodate the whole person growing inside it. My breasts were heavier, fuller, with dark green veins traced across them like vines growing beneath my skin. My face was dotted with hormonal acne, as was my chest; my stomach bowed out at the waist and a dark line ran from my bellybutton to my pubic bone, cutting me down the middle. Extra weight clung to my thighs and my hands and feet were slightly puffier, like someone had blown a mouthful of air into a surgical glove.

Evaluating myself with such scrutiny, I was surprised to find that not one overwhelming emotion rose to the surface. I felt a mixture of things: awe and pride at what my body had accomplished, disgust and discomfort with how much it had changed, regret at my overindulgence during pregnancy and fear that I'd seen the last of my old body. In one breath I gave myself grace for having just housed and birthed a baby—*of course my body wouldn't look the same immediately*—and in the next berated myself for not being able to control this one part of my life when so much else had changed. Every time I looked in the mirror for months following my first son's birth, I experienced this emotional tug-of-war. It was enough to give a person whiplash.

I'd loved my pregnant body. Though I'd always been athletic and had exercised off and on for most of my pregnancy, I'd also allowed myself to indulge in a way I hadn't for probably a decade without feeling an ounce of guilt. During the years of my eating disorder, I often longed to be pregnant just so I could finally lay down the yoke of constantly having to stay thin. When I finally got pregnant many years later, I refused to let myself feel shame or disgust about the changes in my body. Rather, I wanted the world to see the evidence of a life growing inside me; that my former prison was now a warm, happy home for my baby. When I finally started showing sometime during my fifth month, I ran out and bought every curve-hugging maternity shirt I could lay my hands on. I didn't mind strangers touching my belly and I welcomed questions about the baby's gender, the name we'd picked out, how I was feeling and when I was due (until around 37 weeks, when I was tired of everything). I got swept up in the magic of it all.

Then I gave birth. It was like the clock struck midnight and I transformed back to Cinderella in her rags, sitting inside a broken down pumpkin surrounded by a bunch of mice. When I left the hospital two days after giving birth, I still looked six months pregnant. My stomach shrunk by the day, but even months later I still had a paunch that felt like it was on full display in all my old clothes. I didn't hate my body, but I was decidedly uncomfortable in it.

I want to tell you some beautiful story about how I grew to love and accept my postpartum body exactly the way it was, because that's what I want for you. But that wouldn't be the truth. The truth is, as much as I respected my body for what it had accomplished, I couldn't make peace with it until it was more like the body I used to know.

Starting around two months postpartum, I began exercising again. At first it was nothing more than a few jumping jacks and squats in my living room while my son played on the floor; then, when I felt strong enough, jogging by myself and, eventually, running with Chase in the jogging stroller. In the beginning, it was only about losing the baby weight—a means to an end. I did see most of it come off, but I also learned that what people had told me about one's body never truly being the same after children was true.

Over time, however, I came to see exercising as a reward for long days of mothering, a way for me to retain some part of my old life that I had enjoyed before having a baby. I'd hit the road and feel total relief at being able to do something just for me, even on the occasions when Chase was in tow. I still indulged when the mood struck—chocolate, pasta and ice cream will always be staples in my diet—but I was snacking less and eating foods I enjoyed that were, for the most part, good for me. I felt strong and healthy and I was really proud of how my body looked.

But I felt like I'd cheated the system. I hadn't learned to accept my body; I'd worked to change it until I was comfortable again. While I was happy with how I looked, I recognized that maybe I was weaker than the women who did the hard work of learning to love and accept their new appearance.

I'm still mired in ambivalence about my postpartum body. After giving birth twice in as many years, I have seen nearly every part of my body morph and change seemingly in hyper speed. Often, I err on the side of rationality. I don't have the time or the ability to work out nearly as often as I did after my first pregnancy and a donut shared with my son at breakfast is much more enjoyable than the hardboiled egg I could be eating instead. Some days, the sight of myself in the mirror is enough to bring tears to my eyes. I will go weeks or months feeling comfortable in my skin and then without notice, those old feelings of shame and disgust will rise up within me, unbidden and unwelcome.

I've done so much work to get to where I am now, but I'm not sure that I'll ever feel 100% at home in my postpartum body. Maybe when I'm past this phase of pregnancy, breastfeeding and constantly shifting hormones, I will settle in and finally learn to love my body without reservation. Or maybe total acceptance just isn't in the cards for me. I truly don't hate my postpartum body. But I don't love it either.

Moms of More Than One: I Get It

Moms of More Than One:

Consider this my formal apology. I'm calling off the dogs, waving the proverbial white flag. If you want, you can say you told me so; I kind of deserve it.

Because, until I became a mother of two kids, *I just didn't get it.*

Prior to my second son's birth, I was still fairly well rested, had relatively decent personal hygiene and ate complete meals with surprising regularity. Honestly, I didn't quite get what all the hype was about never eating, sleeping or showering again. I was proud that I'd beaten the odds and, somehow, retained a pretty decent amount of my old life in the face of new motherhood.

And then I had a second baby and, suddenly, the truth behind all those memes about moms mainlining coffee and hiding in the bathroom scarfing stashed-away chocolate became very clear to me.

I finally get it. I get all of it.

I get why the TV is always on, even though you once swore you'd never be one of those parents who uses Dora as a babysitter. Why the attractiveness of 23 minutes of slightly subdued children outweighs the nagging guilt you feel over filling their brains with animated garbage.

I get how you go from freezing big batches of organic, homemade purees for your firstborn to stocking your pantry with 10 for $10 Gerber jars to feed your second baby. How you wind up slapping some peanut butter on a slice of stale bread and calling it a meal instead of the artfully constructed lunches you once made when there was still time for things like cutting up carrot sticks.

I get the sudden realization that one of your children is the dirty kid in class (you know the one I'm talking about) because the crusty dried milk above his lip and the remains of a car seat breakfast are somehow overlooked while hustling two kids into daycare.

I get how even the best of routines go off the rails; how baths are foregone, teeth remain unbrushed, pages in the bedtime books are skipped. How you and your spouse convene on the couch after finally wrangling all the kids into bed ("I said that was the last glass of water!" "No, I don't know where your lamby is!") and think, "Where the hell did the last two hours of my life go?"

I get why you give in to the temper tantrum, why you dispense a snack for a moment of peace and quiet, why you hand over your phone if it means you can get through the pediatrician appointment without a five alarm meltdown. (I really, deeply vowed I'd never be *that* parent. Foot, meet mouth.)

I get how it can start to feel like you only work to pay daycare or that it would be easier and more efficient if you just handed your entire paycheck directly to Target. How the lifestyle that seemed tight with one kid feels, at times, downright impossible with more. (Did you know that kids have to eat every day? Apparently, they do.)

I get how the makeup suddenly goes untouched, the cute little dress stays on the hanger and the novel sits unfinished on the nightstand, bookmarked on page 18 for all eternity. How you realize one day that you don't recognize a single song on the radio anymore or that, lately, the only news you consume comes from Facebook and looks a lot more like a picture of someone's brunch than anything truly newsworthy. #nomnom

I get why you are perpetually, chronically, abhorrently late to every single thing, despite your best intentions. Why leaving the house seems like the answer to all your problems until you spend the better part of an hour packing contingency snacks, searching for the always misplaced shoe and nursing the baby who is predictably starving right after she's strapped in the car seat. And why, suddenly, it makes so much more sense to just never go anywhere ever again.

I get how tempers are quicker to ignite, patience runs dry faster and anger rears its ugly head more often than you'd like. I get how, despite the deep and all-consuming way you love your children, some days it feels like you're merely surviving motherhood instead of enjoying it.

Like I said, I get it all.

But here's what I also get: that, despite the worry that you could never love another baby like your first, your heart morphs and expands to include every one of your children the moment they are born. That your love for each one takes a slightly different shape, but is equally fierce and proportionately profound. That, even on the days when it feels like you're doing life blindfolded with both hands tied behind your back, you will never be happier than in this seems-like-forever-but—is-really-just-a-moment whirlwind of raising children. And, that, having more kids is, in fact, not the end of life as you know it, but really just the beginning of a life that's different, but far better.

Sincerely,

A mom of two who finally gets it

The Runaway Mommy

Every now and then, when my day home with the kids is particularly trying, I dream of running away.

Usually it's not somewhere exotic or even new to me; I don't envision a trip to Fiji or a jaunt through Venice. I'm much more practical about the whole thing. I picture myself nabbing the only remaining couch spot at Starbucks or sitting with a $7 glass of Cabernet in an anonymous bar a few towns over.

I plot my escape like one would plan a retirement: sensibly, methodically, unemotionally. In my mind I'm not just sprinting off into the growing darkness that lies beyond the front door with no idea how I'm going to get past the end of our cul-de-sac. No, I have a plan. I am a mom, after all.

First, I will make sure the kids are fed, because God knows, they're impossible to reason with if they're even marginally hungry. The older one will need at least a half dozen snacks to get through the next 45 minutes and the baby will eat continuously for hours on end. Before I go, I'll need to pump a sufficient supply of milk—maybe around 80 ounces—that'll buy me at least enough time to get past the town line. I'll have to locate the yellow sippy cup—NOT the blue one—and make sure there are several gallons of whole milk on hand. Otherwise the wheels will fall off the operation pretty quickly.

Then I will have to tidy up the house; I really hate coming home to a mess. I'll make sure the dishes are washed and dried, the playroom is straightened up and all the laundry is folded. While I'm folding the laundry, I'll notice that the bathroom floor hasn't been washed in weeks and while I'm mopping it, I'll see the toothpaste-splattered sink and the water-spotted vanity mirror. There will be a handful of toys in the bathtub that need to be put away and, when I'm bent over the tub, I'll discover the contents of my makeup bag in the bathroom trash. All this tidying up will take me until approximately the following Tuesday to accomplish, by conservative estimates, but it's OK; I'm in no rush.

Of course, I will need to attend to the matter of their clothes— it wouldn't feel right leaving that task for someone else to tackle. Each of them will go through roughly three outfits per day, not accounting for external factors like a painting activity or spaghetti night, so I'll leave four, just to be safe. The older one will want the socks that don't go past his ankles and the baby will need a few clean bibs, otherwise his outfit count will be more like six or seven for the day. It's likely that someone will leak through his diaper, so a couple sets of clean sheets and the blanket that looks *almost* the same as the older one's favorite will need to be ready for a middle-of-the-night emergency.

The diaper bag should probably be stocked, too. I'll add the diapers and wipes, bibs and burp cloths, the pacifier that the baby hasn't used in six months, but could want at any moment.

I'll make sure there are extra outfits, including socks and shoes, snacks and a water bottle, hand sanitizer and some Tylenol in case someone spikes a fever. The bag will weigh a ton but better to be safe than sorry. I'm almost ready to go now; just need to lay out their pajamas and turn the sound machine to the right setting, oh and set the thermostat to the 71 degrees to which the boys have grown accustomed.

Before I go I'll just sit down for a minute because I'm kind of tired and I could use a second to relax before I make my big getaway. I'll settle onto the couch, ease back the recliner, pull out my phone for some mindless News Feed scrolling. Just as I'm about to fire up Facebook, a little person will come ambling over and climb up into my lap. Without a word, he'll settle himself into my chest, his hair ticking my chin, that little boy smell wafting off him. He'll idly trace patterns on my jeans with his fingers, cozy his perpetually-warm feet under my legs. I'll kiss the top of his head and he'll sink back into me, his heat warming me, his little body finally still for the first time all day.

Maybe my trip can wait, I'll think. I can always run away tomorrow.

If a Tree Falls In the Woods...

The ATM inside the Cumberland Farms gas station is no more than 20 feet from my Jeep, which is parked just outside the front of the store. It's 9:45 a.m. on a Thursday—the part of the day that's safely sandwiched between the morning rush and lunchtime—so there are only a handful of other patrons present, some pumping gas, others running inside for a pack of smokes or a mid-morning Red Bull.

I weigh my options: I can extract each child from his respective car seat and haul them both inside for the 13 seconds it will take me to swipe my card, agree to the exorbitant transaction fee and collect my twenty dollar bill; or I can leave them sleeping in the back, lock them safely inside and use the remote starter to keep the air conditioner running while I watch from the window.

I've never done this before—actually gone through with it— but I've thought about it maybe a thousand times. About how much easier it would be to just run inside and leave them in the car while I buy the one item I left off my shopping list. About forgoing the 27-step process of successfully entering and exiting a store with two small children in favor of a three-minute transaction. Every time, when push came to shove, I just couldn't bring myself to leave them, for any number of reasons. Because my older son might wake up and realize I'm not there. Because the air-conditioned car might suddenly overheat. Because someone could hot-wire my SUV in those 90 seconds and drive off with my most precious cargo in tow.

But the biggest reason I never went through with it?

The fear that a perfect stranger would see my children strapped into their car seats through the tinted windows and, upon my return, berate me for endangering them. Or worse, call the police and recount for their benefit how I put my children in harm's way.

In this moment, sitting in the driver's seat analyzing these absurd potential outcomes, I realize just how much I let the fear of being deemed a bad mother by total strangers dictate the way I publicly parent my own children.

Which, naturally, leads to me to wonder: what type of parent would I be if no one were watching?

I'm genuinely curious. Would I be the type that didn't weigh the bunch of bananas at the grocery store before letting my older son devour one? Would I be the type that didn't keep up a constant stream of chatter with my very disinterested infant for the sole benefit of complete strangers? Or would my infractions be more serious? Would I be the type that drank a glass of wine and nursed my suddenly starving baby in front of a restaurant full of people? Would I be the type that confidently fed my firstborn Enfamil instead of suffering through five long months of exclusive pumping just to avoid judgment?

If I were being brutally, unabashedly honest, I'd answer yes to every single one of those questions. And, if no one was watching, I wouldn't even feel bad about it.

That, of course, begs the question: why do I let total strangers have so much sway over my decision-making as a mother?

I think it's more than just one easy, cookie cutter answer; it's a lot of little factors that make me so wary of going with my gut and doing what I think is best for my children. Part of it is that we are living in a time of swift and unyielding judgment, where we as parents are put on trial in the court of public opinion seemingly every moment of our lives. Someone is always waiting to tell us that we were wrong, that they know better, that, in the same circumstance, they would have made the right choice (and yes, there is always a right choice, which just so happens to be the one we didn't make).

Another part of it is that a judgmental stranger sees only a snapshot of my life as a mother, not the whole lovingly compiled photo album. It's the reason I look over my shoulder when I hand my phone to Chase during a meltdown in a restaurant or let him eat McDonald's in the stands at his father's softball game: because I always said I'd never do things like that and I fear being criticized for my split-second decision.

I don't want to be the type of person who particularly cares what other people think. And yet the fact remains: for me, fear of judgment has an undue influence on the choices I make as a mother.

So when I march into the gas station and hastily punch the buttons on the ATM—fast cash, no receipt—I worry the entire two minutes. Not about my children safely cocooned in the backseat of an air conditioned car, but about the passenger in parking spot next to mine who is mere feet away from discovering my secret. Were she not there, I'm confident that I'd have no qualms about my choice. But there she is, completely unaware—of my children in the backseat, of the internal struggle I'm wrestling with inside the Cumberland Farms, of her unwitting role in the decision I've made now and will in the future. And there I am, just 20 feet away, with a hair-trigger paranoia making it seem much farther. Once again, I've let myself get caught up in what a total stranger thinks of me as a mother.

Which, naturally, begs the question: If a mom leaves her child in a safely-locked car and no one else is around to judge her, does she still question her decision?

The Full

My coat pockets are stuffed with used wipes. There's a blanket of crushed Goldfish and limbless Teddy Grahams covering the floor of my Jeep. My wallet is crammed with receipts for things I'll never return: a half-used lip gloss, a quarter tank of gas, a drive-thru muffin I've already consumed. Of course, it contains none of the receipts I actually need.

The sink is piled high with crusty dishes and the dishwasher is full again; no one remembered to run it last night. The hampers are overflowing and the dryer can't accommodate one more load. The recycling bin is no longer accepting new milk cartons, the Diaper Genie is maxed out and the kitchen trashcan is one banana peel away from a revolt.

My phone keeps alerting me that there's not enough space for one more photo—it doesn't care that the baby is looking especially adorable today. There's a waiting line for the DVR and no one is getting in, no matter how enticing she seems (I'm looking at you, *New Girl*.) My inbox is on the verge of implosion.

There are so many days when my life feels too full. Full to the brim. Full to capacity. Full to bursting. All I want is fewer. Thoughts in my brain. Bills in the pile. Appointments on the calendar.

I long for the simple. The straightforward. The empty. I wonder if there will ever come a day when I will be caught up on all that's outstanding; the myriad tasks that just never seem finished no matter how often they're done.

"How is it possible that the trashcan gets this full in two days?" I inquire of my husband several times per week.

It's rhetorical, but I really do want to know. As I stand before the sink with water-shriveled skin, I contemplate how it can take thirty minutes to get to the bottom of the stack of dishes and three minutes to fill it to the top again. Each time I begin folding yet another tiny tee shirt I absently wonder, *Will I ever find the bottom of the laundry pile or is empty just an illusion?*

Full is usually positive. We all want full hair. Full bellies. Full hearts. I'm happiest when many aspects of my life are full, especially my wine glass and my wallet. But, sometimes, full is too much. I find myself full of stress. Impatience. Anxiety. All at once, everything is overflowing, overwhelming. Bursting, breaking, busting at the seams.

I love the full. Right up until I don't anymore.

Recently, I was commiserating with a girlfriend about our too-full lives. We are both the type that habitually bites off more than she can chew then wonders how she wound up drowning in the stress of too many obligations. "I want to book two solid nights in the resort by my house and drink at the bar and order room service and go to the spa and not speak to one fucking person I don't have to for two full days," she said. "I'm just tapped. Completely tapped out."

I know exactly how she feels. Constantly wondering when that little something will finally give. When the full will officially become too much to bear.

But then there's the empty. A word that, at times, seems so tantalizing. An empty schedule. Empty sink. Empty dryer. Empty purse. Empty mind. I want so badly to experience empty for just one day; 24 hours where everything is clear and simple and uncluttered.

But I know empty has a dark side. By its very definition, it's devoid of, deficient in, lacking something. *Empty promises. Empty wallet. Empty arms.* The substance is missing, the life drained out.

The full is hectic and stressful and crazy-making, but it's also beautiful and rich and alive. It's muddy shoes in the entryway and petrified spaghetti in the garbage disposal, backpacks abandoned on couches and smudgy fingerprints on the stainless steel. It's evidence of life—a life packed with so much substance, it's ready to burst at the seams.

The empty is so enticing. It's quiet houses and clear schedules, a fresh start, a clean slate. When the full becomes too much, the empty is a comforting notion, a pleasant daydream.

But it's just that: a dream, an illusion. Because the full is messy and complicated, but it's also tangible and real. The proof is stacked and smushed and crammed and piled all around me. It's the thing that makes it all worth it.

How lucky I am to have a life so full.

The Gift of Not Being Able to Breastfeed

I cried nearly every time Chase was awake for the first three weeks of his life.

Incidentally, he was usually crying too, but for very different reasons; him because he was starving and me because I didn't have enough milk to keep him from starving. Every time he woke and frantically sought nourishment from nipples that left bloody stains on the front of my t-shirt, I fervently wished he would go back to sleep and leave my nipples alone. There was nothing successful about our breastfeeding endeavor: I was in excruciating pain and he was not being fed to the point of satiation. The weight of my failure as a mother and a woman was crushing.

Countless lactation appointments shed some light on the problem: Chase was receiving barely any milk upon feeding. I'd sit in the windowless office at the hospital, nursing him for 20 minutes on each side, then anxiously await the news that he'd taken in barely half an ounce after eating for the better part of an hour. In his frustration at not getting enough milk, he'd thrash his little head back and forth, tearing apart my already ravaged nipples and causing me agonizing pain. For weeks he'd been constantly hungry, unless he managed to fall asleep for a blessed stretch of time, during which I'd count down the minutes until he'd need to eat again. I saw myself falling headlong into depression. How could I ever learn to enjoy motherhood when I was failing at the most basic duty of being a mother?

Chase wasn't gaining enough weight from breastfeeding alone, so his pediatrician suggested formula supplementation as a solution. I decided, instead, to opt for exclusive pumping; I'd been told that with the right combination of around-the-clock pumping and temporary insanity I'd be able to successfully increase my supply. I pumped every two hours for five months. At certain times of the day I'd sit hooked up to the pump for an hour straight in an effort to simulate cluster feeding. Chase began sleeping through the night at six weeks, but I was awake in the wee hours of every morning pumping, cleaning and storing, bent at the waist watching the agonizingly slow drip of breast milk plink into the bottles.

Even with my absurd regimen of Mother's Milk tea, Fenugreek, gallons of water, lactation cookies (OK, I enjoyed those) and seemingly nonstop pumping, my supply never increased. I began to supplement little by little, unable to keep up with my son's voracious appetite, literally pumping one minute to feed it to him the next. One day when he was nearing five months old I decided enough was enough. I started to space out the daytime pumping sessions, cut out the nighttime ones altogether and prepared for the guilt I would feel throwing in the towel on breastfeeding for good.

In the beginning, I did experience my fair share of guilt. But the overriding emotion I felt? Relief. So why in God's name would I be happy to have experienced all of that?

Simple: because it makes me understand that there are two sides to the breastfeeding coin. That, despite what we're told, sometimes it just doesn't work the way it's supposed to.

If breastfeeding had always been relatively smooth (I say relatively because I don't think it's necessarily a walk in the park for any woman), I would not have understood how momentous it is to watch your child grow and thrive as a direct result of your nourishment. Yet I feel conflicted. I am equal parts proud of the fact that I've been able to breastfeed my second baby and a traitor to those women who feel the way I did the first time: frustrated, failed, useless.

If this second time had always been my experience—an adequate milk supply, an eager feeder with a proper latch, strong lactation support to guide me through the rough patches— I might have ended up being the type of woman who stands on her soapbox chanting "breast is best" and deriding another woman's choice to formula feed. I sort of get how that happens. Knowing you can nourish your child from your own body is a heady feeling and doing it successfully is a badge of honor. Couple that with the fact that it's usually difficult at the start and there are often several hurdles to overcome before true success and you've got the perfect recipe for a superiority complex. I have to assume that these women who are always on their high horses about breastfeeding have gotten so caught up in the emotional side of it that they lose their minds when it comes to how other women choose to feed their babies. I'll never know for sure, but maybe my experience kept me from becoming one of them.

My experience has also instilled a built-in sensitivity in me about breastfeeding; because I have had every designation possible— an exclusive pumper, a formula feeder and, finally, a successful breastfeeder—I am hyper aware of the fact that there is no "right" way to feed a child. Now I sit in my weekly breast-feeding support group and watch as other women struggle with the same news I once received: that their child isn't gaining as quickly as they should, that something has broken down in this system that's supposed to come so naturally. I feel for them be-cause I've been there; sitting in a circle of moms, wondering why I seem to be the only one whose body has failed her, scanning for judgmental looks as I pull out a bottle of formula while their babies all nurse contentedly. It's made me realize that sometimes breastfeeding doesn't come as easily as it has this time. It gives me an appreciation of my experience breastfeeding Sam that I'd never have gained absent my struggles with Chase.

It seems there is a confluence of factors that must be present for successful breastfeeding—some physical, some emotional, some social—and, because of my first experience, I realize that sometimes these just don't converge. More than that, I realize that it's OK when they don't. There is so much more to being a good mother than breastfeeding.

To My Boys

Chase and Sam,

Right now you are still so little, both of you just babies in the grand scheme of things. Adulthood is no more than a hazy thought that seems lifetimes removed from the phase we're in now; this era of endless diapers, sticky hands and bedtime snuggles. Many days, firmly ensconced as we are in this stage, I can convince myself that you will never grow up, that you'll stay my little boys forever. In fact, I often beg you to, whispering the plea in your tiny ears while you're watching television or rocking with me before bed. I take your silence as an agreement to remain this age indefinitely.

I know it doesn't quite work that way. At some point you will surpass me in height, you'll grow enough facial hair to warrant shaving, you'll start

seeing girls in your class as more than just sparkly pink mysteries covered in cooties. When that
time comes, there are things I want you to know
about life, about love, about what's important and
what's not worth your worry.

First of all, listen to your mother. I may not
always make sense to you—just a grown up version of a sparkly pink cootie-covered mystery—
but I have a little more life experience under my
belt and I want you to learn from my mistakes (of
which there are many). When you are in doubt
about the kind of man you hope to be someday,
look to your father—he is the single best example
of dedication, loyalty, hard work and uncondi-
tional love you could ever hope to model your-
selves after. Though I've always admired and
respected him, he became even more worthy of
my admiration and respect when he became your
father. Don't even give a thought to trying to divide us against each other; we are a united front
and, even when we don't agree on things, we support each other without question.

Learn to become somewhat self-sufficient
before you are out on your own in the world.
Practice how to make a bed, fold a shirt, iron a
collar, load a dishwasher. Be careful with your
money and understand that credit card debt
will follow you around much longer than you
will enjoy 20% off of the newest gaming system
from Best Buy. Knowing how to make a few basic
(and not-so-basic) meals that involve more than

pressing start on the microwave will serve you well (and impress prospective girlfriends, too). And, for the love of God, make sure you aim and put the seat down afterward.

Remember that every person you meet deserves respect. Not just your parents and your spouse, but your coworkers, the cashier at the drugstore, and the woman you accidentally bump into on the train. The person you end up with is someone who should command your respect, but remember that you should give it freely, regardless.

Be a class act. Don't blow snot rockets on the football field or adjust your manhood in a public place. Keep your bodily functions to yourself when possible and, if you just can't help it, at least say excuse me.

Though I'd like to believe it, I am not so naïve to think you will wait until marriage to have sex. Understand that sex is not the casual act that some make it out to be; it is a momentous decision that should not be taken lightly by either you or the other person. No always means no. Listening and obeying that command is a form of respect, which, as I've already mentioned, is non-negotiable in any relationship. Use protection (more than one form, if possible) and let the person you choose as your first be worthy of sharing that milestone. You only have one first and it's something you will both remember all of your lives.

Do not expect the world to fall at your feet. To your father and I, you are special and perfect, but not everyone will agree with that sentiment. Throughout your life you will encounter tyrants and bullies, people who will derive pleasure from attempting to make you feel small. Do not give them the satisfaction. You are the only person who can determine your own worth and only you have the power to allow someone else's actions to make you feel any certain way. Be a humble winner and a gracious loser. Cheer for the underdog and help those who are in a tough spot—you never know when that will be you.

Understand that you are fortunate to have the life you do and do not take it for granted. Some are not so lucky. The house you live in, the car that gets you where you need to go, the food you consume endlessly: those things are luxuries, not rights. Someday, you will have to work hard for those comforts yourself, but right now, your father and I provide them freely. A thank you every now and then goes a long way. And don't forget to thank the Big Guy Upstairs: He's the one who makes it all happen.

Stick together. A sibling is one of the greatest gifts you could be fortunate enough to receive. I know you will fight—it's just part of growing up alongside someone, especially someone so close in age—but remember to fight for each other when the stakes are high. God willing, you will be here together long after your dad and I are gone, and you will need each other to weather the tough times and celebrate the good times. If you're the best man at your brother's wedding, *do not get drunk before you give your speech.* Trust me on that one. Family is more important than anything; if you remember nothing else of what I've taught you, remember that.

Get to know and like yourself. You'll be spending a lot of time with you over the years and you should be the type of person with whom you'd want to be friends. Don't be afraid to have preferences and be firm about what you like—you can do that without being pushy or difficult. Sometimes you will have to do things to appease those you love, like go to a restaurant you don't particularly care for or sit through a sixth grade saxophone concert, but those small sacrifices will be worth it to please the people who mean the most to you. In those instances, don't complain. Be thankful that someone loves you enough to want to spend time with you.

Tell your wife you love her every single day. More importantly, show your love in ways that let her know how much you care, even when you're not actually saying the words. You will weather seemingly insurmountable odds and impossible differences throughout your marriage. At times it will feel like the best choice is to give up. Don't. Remember why you chose that person in the first place and honor your commitment to love and respect each other, even on the days when you don't particularly like one another.

Don't be scared of becoming a parent some-day. There will be plenty of naysayers who will warn you of the sleep you'll lose and the free time that will evaporate. They are right, of course, but they're not telling you the whole story. Being a parent is, without a doubt, the greatest thing you can achieve in your lifetime. It is fulfilling and life-affirming in ways you cannot begin to imagine now. Yes, it is also exhausting and frustrating and some days it will take every fiber of your being to keep from completely losing your head, but it is worth it. My God, is it worth it.

Above all else, remember that I love you. With a madness and ferocity you couldn't possibly comprehend until you have a child of your own. There is nothing on this earth that could keep me from you when you need me, no argument or difference of opinion that would change the love I have for you. I will advocate for you, stand behind you, guide you gently and slap you upside the head when you need it. And, someday, I will love you enough to send you off to make your own way in the world. When that day comes, take what I've told you here to heart. Just remember: always listen to your mother.

With love,

Mom

A Tribe Called Mom

There have been so many times as a new mom that I've found myself blind-sided by the utter loneliness of motherhood. The other night, the baby was up nearly every hour. Each time I heard the monitor come to life with his howls and wails, I reluctantly climbed out of my warm bed and trudged down the hall to retrieve him from his crib, change his diaper and settle with him in the rocking chair. Upon latching him on to nurse, he immediately calmed then became too sleepy to eat. Back in his crib he went and inevitably woke as soon as I laid down in my own bed with barely enough time to pull the comforter over me. On and on it went all night and into the early hours of the morning.

With the baby still hungrily sucking at me as the sun came up over the trees, all I could manage to feel was bone-deep exhaustion and overwhelming loneliness. Adam is as involved as they come—helpful and engaged almost to the point of too-good-to-be-true—but after several attempts at rocking Sam while he frantically gnawed on the front of Adam's tee shirt, my husband had no choice but to pass him off to me, the only one who could give him what he wanted. As I gazed at this frustrating little person we'd created while my husband slept soundly beside me, I was consumed by my loneliness. I knew there were thousands, maybe millions, of mothers awake with children at that exact moment, but they were down the street or several continents removed and I was here, by myself with an infant who cried for a reason I couldn't diagnose.

The next day I took my two boys to the local library for story time. When we got there I was pleasantly surprised to see a good friend of ours sitting cross-legged on the rug with two of her three kids. We whispered of our shared exhaustion between renditions of "Wheels on the Bus" and "If You're Happy and You Know It" (we were not) and, instantly, I felt the burden of a bad night lift from my shoulders. I was not alone. Someone else had been there too. It gave me comfort that even my husband could not have provided.

We spent the rest of our morning together chatting about the common ground of motherhood: leaky boobs and coffee dependencies, mothers-in-law and pediatrician recommendations. To an outsider, it would just seem like idle chit chat to fill the silence between, "Don't put that in your mouth!" and "Give that toy back to him!" But to me it was a lifeline. I desperately needed to give voice to my frustration and exhaustion because to do so made it feel less huge, less all-consuming. If someone else I knew was going through it too, it meant I wasn't alone in feeling the way I did.

Had someone asked me right before Chase was born what I thought was the biggest necessity for having a new baby, I'd probably have said a crib or a car seat. Maybe a few sets of one-piece pajamas or a receiving blanket. If asked now? I would not hesitate a second before answering, "I need a friend." Prior to having kids, I'd heard other moms talk about finding their "tribe." Part of me scoffed, thinking that I wouldn't really need new friends. Even though my old ones weren't yet mothers, I knew I wouldn't become one of those women who abandons all her friends once she has a baby. And I didn't—I see a lot of my childless friends on a regular basis and we still have a great time together on those occasions. But having mom friends is something else entirely, something crucial to survival as a new mother.

The only problem was I had no idea how to go about finding brand new friends. I'd had many of the same friends since college and I wasn't accustomed to meeting new people outside the world of bars and house parties. I wasn't shy or (too) socially awkward, but the idea of having to start over was daunting, to say the least. As one of my friends put it recently, "It's kind of like middle school all over again." She's not wrong. Sometimes when I sit in a mommy and me class surrounded by other moms I don't know yet, I get the familiar feeling of being 12-years-old, staring shyly at the boy I like in homeroom, trying to get up the courage to ask him out on a date. (And by "date," I mean my dad drives both of us to the movies and I sit in the dark awkwardly holding his sweaty hand for ninety minutes. But I digress.)

Out on walks with my firstborn, I'd see clusters of moms pushing strollers in the park and wonder how they'd come to know each other. Was there some secret place to meet other moms that no one had told me about? Did I somehow miss the signup sheet for mom friends? I'd go to these classes at the hospital where my son was delivered and think, *I'm bound to meet some-one I click with in a room full of other new moms.*

But then a strange thing would happen: we'd each be sitting cross-legged on the floor mere inches from the nearest mom, babbling in high-pitched voices to our respective babies, completely ignoring each other. Sure, there would be a mom or two chatting here and there, but for the most part the adults stayed engrossed in the routine tasks of motherhood—breastfeeding, diaper changing, facilitating tummy time—until the hour was up and it was time to schlep back to our lonely houses. I went religiously every week, desperate for an excuse to get out, but nothing ever changed.

Until one day when I decided I just couldn't take the silence anymore. I sat next to these moms every single week (and had seen most of their nipples) but had yet to so much as introduce myself. So I hoisted up my big girl pants, turned to one of them and began with that familiar new mom question: "How old is your baby?" Not an inspired query, I realize, but it got the proverbial ball rolling.

Suddenly we were actually talking. *To each other.* It was a thing of beauty. We chatted about diaper brands and I asked where she'd gotten her nursing cover. The conversation stayed at the surface level, but at least we were finally doing more than sitting in shared silence. Still, when it came time to leave, there was an awkward dance of pleasantries, followed by me exiting the hospital no closer to having a new friend than when I entered. *Why didn't I just ask if she wanted to get together for a playdate?* I thought. *Next week. I'll definitely ask her next week.*

It took me far too long to get up the courage to ask any of those moms to do something outside of the hospital classes, but eventually I bit the bullet and extended an invitation to get together at the park. Each time I did it, making the first move got easier. One of the women from that group is still a good friend to this day. Some of them I didn't particularly connect with; we'd hang out once or twice, but it wouldn't materialize into a lasting friendship. It was much like playing the field when you're dating: feeling the other person out, asking questions to see if there are compatibility issues, wondering if you'll make the cut for a second (play) date. Every time I'd see another mom with kids that looked to be about the same age as mine, I'd think, *This could be my person*. I'd wasted a lot of time already letting potential friends get away. At some point I realized I'd never make friends if I didn't just get out there and introduce myself to the moms who seemed to be everywhere I looked.

After I'd known some of these other moms for a while, we'd eventually get around to talking about the first time we met. Just the other day a now good friend of mine said, "I thought you were so pretty and you looked so great after just having a baby," referring to our first meeting in an infant/toddler swim class. Oddly enough, I remember watching her chatting comfortably with another woman in the class (who is also a friend of mine now) and thinking, "They seem like people I'd get along with, but they already know each other. I guess they probably don't need new friends as badly as I do." At the time, my son was six months old and we had just moved back to our hometown after being gone for almost a decade. All of my high school friends had moved away and I was essentially starting from scratch in the friends department. I figured these women were already established here with plenty of mom friends and it wasn't likely they were looking for more.

As it turns out, I couldn't have been more wrong. We were all just as desperate to make more friends, but each of us was too shy to be the first to doing anything about it.

Every now and then I ask the women who follow One Mother to Another about their mom friends. Most say they have one or two or none at all. Many say they don't know where to find them or how to start the conversation when they do. Others say they feel judged because they're much younger or much older than the other moms with kids their child's age or because they use cloth diapers or bottle-feed or have a hand-me-down stroller.

But the common thread amongst their answers? They all desire more mom friends. Not a single one has ever said she has enough and isn't in the market for more, *thankyouverymuch*. What their answers tell me is that we all seem to crave connection with each other and yet are so afraid of rejection, we're content just not to try. But so much is lost if we don't, because how will we ever find our tribes if we don't extend ourselves?

The other day I was chatting with a woman at our church. She has two young sons—one right around Chase's age. I'd talked to her before for a minute or two between services as she and her family were coming and we were going, but nothing extensive. I liked her. I could see that we might make good friends. I didn't know anything about how many mom friends she already has in her circle or whether she wanted a new one, but I decided it was time I extended myself for once. "Let's get the boys together for a play date sometime," I said. She smiled. "We'd love to. That would be great." She began listing off their availability, putting the wheels of our budding friendship in motion. I could tell she meant it when she said they'd love to get together.

We might meet up once and decide it isn't a good fit. Or maybe in six years we'll be at our monthly girls' night out, talking about the day we first met while we gossip and make our way through our customary pitcher of sangria. I have no idea what the future holds for our friendship, but I am positive of how it would play out if I'd never made the first move.

Though there are still times when I hesitate to be the first to reach out—like just the other day when I was chatting with another mom about sippy cups in Wal-Mart and I let her leave without asking for her number—I'm much bolder now than I once was. It's not that I've developed some unflinching confidence I didn't have before; it's more that I recognize how awkward it is for everyone, not just me. I know now that you can't tell how many friends another mom has just by looking at her and that most women would love to have another friend, if given the opportunity. I realize that if I want another one of my own, I might just have to be the first person to say so.

Lately, I've been trying like hell to find my tribe; a group of women who will take me exactly as I am, even though I forget to answer text messages, rarely wash my floors and show up horrifically late to every single play date. I'm on constant alert for those kindred mom spirits I know are out there: in the grocery aisles, at the library story time, on the playground, at the YMCA pool. I make small talk, give compliments and exchange numbers, in the hopes that one of them will end up becoming the friend I've been waiting for. If I never end up finding my tribe, it won't be because I didn't try.

Judgment Day

Before my sons were born and I became a stay-at-home-mom, I worked in childcare centers for several years. I taught nearly every age, bouncing from classroom to classroom and center to center before eventually winding up in management at a couple of different schools. I was young—newly married and still in my early 20s—but I truly thought I knew it all. I was certain of exactly the type of parent I'd never be when I had children of my own. I had real, live case studies to prove that most parents had little idea of what was best for their children.

The mom that packed Easy Mac and Goldfish in her three year old's lunchbox every single day? There was no way I'd be her. My husband and I ate almost completely organic and mostly Paleo; all leafy greens and free-range chicken breasts, non-GMO apples and cage-free eggs. Sure, our grocery bill was astronomical for two people, but it was worth every penny. Our kids' diets would never include a laundry list of toxins; hell, they wouldn't even *know* what Easy Mac was because I'd never be lazy enough to put that on the table in front of them. The mom who rocked her two-year-old son to sleep every night then literally crawled across the floor so as not to wake him upon her exit? Ridiculous. I wouldn't even consider coddling my child that way. I knew the value in teaching children independence and self-sufficiency early; in creating positive, healthy sleep habits that definitely did not include hour-long bedtime rituals.

Right after I got pregnant with Chase, I received an email from a family member with the link to an article about the types of things you say you'll never do until you become a parent. I was affronted. There might be people who change their philosophies and ideals when they have children, but I was certainly not going to be one of them. I knew how detrimental some of those behaviors were to young children and there was no way I'd waffle on my principles in the face of a screaming toddler. She clearly didn't know me very well if she assumed I'd just cave like that.

You see where this is going, right?

Not too long ago, I found myself propped up next to my older son's crib, rubbing his back through the narrow slats as he hiccuped with barely-contained tears. For reasons unknown to me, he went from being a champion sleeper to waking up three or four times per night, starting almost immediately after being put in his crib. This latest chorus of tears began just minutes after Adam sat down on the couch having just put him in bed for the second time that night. "I'll go up this time," I offered reluctantly. Upon opening the door, I found Chase thrashing and kicking, emitting high-pitched screams like the frighteningly loud Fisher Cats that took up nighttime residence in the woods behind our house. He did not want to be sung to or rocked. He refused a cup of water. He just wanted to be in his crib under his blue blanket, clutching his bear, with me beside him, rubbing small circles over his tiny back. How could I deny him that comfort? And, of course, as I sat there with my right butt cheek going numb and my arm wedged uncomfortably through the crib rails, preparing for my soundless exit from the room wherein I would crawl to the door Army-style, it hit me like a ton of bricks: *How the mighty have fallen.*

I was never going to be the type of parent who used television as a babysitter. Now my son knows the names of the characters on Super Why better than some of his family members and learned to recite the theme song before his ABCs.

I was never going to be the type of parent who allowed her children to eat anywhere other than the table or used food as a bribe for good behavior. Now, my kids eats nearly everywhere but the table and snacks have become a form of currency: *Do this for me and I'll give you a graham cracker. Do it without pouting and I'll throw in a second.*

I was never going to be the type of parent who let her personal space become overrun with toys and kid paraphernalia. Now, my living room looks like Fisher-Price vomited in it and my car has become a breeding ground for stale granola bar remnants and dirty onesies.

I was never going to be the type of parent who fed her children "kid food" or let herself become a short order cook; if they were hungry enough, they'd eat whatever I made for them. Now Chase eats peanut butter and jelly sandwiches for lunch nearly every day and I find myself cooking a separate dinner more often than I'd care to admit. (It's a lot. Like, *a lot* a lot.)

The type of parent I thought I was going to be would've been such an asshole.

Recently, I was discussing this very fact with a friend of mine with whom I worked at one of those daycare centers. At the time, we'd both been childless and full of opinions about how to raise other people's children. Our most often used phrase in those days was something to the effect of, "If that were my kid..." followed by some groundbreaking solution that the child's parent clearly had not yet considered. We were "sanctimommies" before the term was coined; in fact, even before becoming mothers ourselves. Of course, now we each have a couple kids of our own and we look back on the judgmental assholes we used to be with total disdain. "We had no clue," my friend said the other day as she relayed a story about her daughter zoning out in front of a Sesame Street marathon while her 37-weeks-pregnant self took a nap. "What was wrong with us?" The truth is, we didn't know better. We believed we would never be at the mercy of a tiny person who would change all our deep-seated beliefs the minute they began throwing a public tantrum. We thought that, when the time came, we'd be different. Stronger. Stricter. More patient. Less indulgent. We thought because we knew better we'd be immune to the pitfalls of so many parents before us.

We were so very wrong.

One by one, each and every rule, expectation and guideline I carefully laid out pre-children has fallen like a row of dominoes. How have I strayed so far from my own principles in such a short period of time? There were certain ones that I stubbornly held onto—fast food, cell phones as a distraction, co-sleeping—until a situation presented itself that left me little other choice: nowhere to eat but McDonalds on a long drive with a hungry toddler, a two-hour wait for a doctor's appointment, a baby who won't sleep unless we're sharing oxygen. I'd feel guilty at first, like I was betraying my younger, more idealistic self, but the next time I'd have to make the same choice—hold the line or surrender in the name of survival—it would feel just a tad easier, slightly more palatable. I had to adapt, and my old ideologies were just not realistic when it came time to put them into practice.

Slowly but surely I was learning an important lesson: when you're in the parenting trenches, you do exactly what you have to do to get through the day. There's no shame in that. Once I gave into the concept of parenting with no hard and fast rules, raising kids began to feel easier. I was free to change my mind and do what worked in the moment without letting anyone down, least of all myself. These days, I am constantly adapting and revising. I do what makes sense at the time and let the expectations fall away. I feel like a better mom without the ghost of my old, judgmental self following me around and pointing out my shortcomings.

Every so often, I'll find myself talking to a brand new or soon-to-be mom and I'll hear her throw around words like "never" and "always;" the type of absolutes I spoke in before I became a mother. She'll talk about how she'll never let her kid eat that certain food or will make sure she always sticks to her guns about that particular habit. A little part of me wants to tell her the truth about what's coming; let her in on one of the best-kept secrets of motherhood. But I never do. I hold back because I remember how offended I was when I opened that email from my well-meaning family member back before I knew she was right. Instead I just smile, hold my tongue and wait it out. I figure in a year or two when we're out to dinner, sipping our wine while our kids watch a movie on those phones we said we'd never let them use, we'll both have a good laugh about what assholes we used to be before we knew better.

If I Stand Up

It's 3:48 p.m. and my toddler is summoning me through the monitor, awake from his nap and pounding so hard against his crib I'm sure it will crash through the ceiling at any moment. The baby lies draped across my lap, out cold, finally asleep for the first time all day. From my position on the couch, I can just see the dishes piled over the lip of the sink, the stack of unopened mail and assorted debris teetering precariously on the kitchen island. The living room curtain is open just far enough that the crack of light coming through shines like a spotlight on the patch of dried spit up that's been caked on the hardwood for over a week, which I somehow seem to miss every time I mop (which is basically never).

For the past thirty minutes I've been sitting in this same spot, trapped between my will to get something—*anything*—done and my desire to soak up these precious moments of my children both sleeping peacefully. If I stand up, I'll have to move the baby off my lap and place him in the bouncy seat where he'll howl and wail until I'm finished changing the toddler's diaper and secur-ing him in his highchair for a snack. I'll sacrifice one child's needs for that of the other, as I so often do, and ask for patience they have not yet developed.

Sometime in the next 20 minutes my husband will text to let me know he's headed home. I'll pull out the ingredients for tonight's dinner and 20 minutes later he'll call to say he's really sorry but he got caught up with his boss and he's just now begin-ning his 35 minute commute and is it OK if he stops real quick to pick up a replacement part for the lawnmower? I'll see my night slipping through my fingertips. There will be diapers changed and snacks dispensed, dishes loaded hastily into the dishwasher, admonitions for the toddler who will snatch the paring knife from the silverware tray and brandish it like a pirate sword. I'll ask him to stop standing on the dishwasher door and then he'll cry and throw himself on the floor when he catches a glimpse of the graham crackers in the pantry and is told he can't eat another because he already had six. Eventually I'll pluck the seventh one out of the brown plastic packaging and thrust it at him angrily, annoyed at him for being annoying, but more annoyed at myself for giving in again.

My mind will swirl with thoughts of unpaid bills, mounting debt and dwindling bank account balances as I dice onions and peel carrots, getting lost in the cathartic effect of cooking, until I realize the toddler is playing with a package of thumbtacks. I'll bounce the baby in one arm and try to keep him as far as possible from the hot pan spitting olive oil, playing out all the possible emergency room trips this situation could produce. I'll think every little sound—the furnace switching on, the wind outside, the sound of the toddler dragging a chair across the floor—is the garage door opening until it actually is and my husband is finally standing here in the kitchen, asking how he can help. He'll take the kids so I can finish dinner, which always takes so much longer than I expect it to, and before I know it we'll be eating just a half hour before the boys should be in bed. The baby will start fussing as soon as I put the plates on the table, so I'll nurse him while trying to eat with my non-dominant hand, dropping crumbs on him with nearly every shaky bite, apologizing as I wipe him off for the fifth time. The meal that took so long to prepare will take approximately four minutes to finish and then we'll split up to get each boy ready for bed (*you want the big one or the little one?*) when all I dream of doing is sitting on the couch and staring into space as I am right now. There will be clothes changed, teeth brushed, an extra TV show negotiated that will draw out the evening but maybe give me extra time to sleep in the morning, and finally they'll both be in their cribs, sure to wake at any moment and summon me through the monitor.

If I stand up, all of this will be set into motion, unfolding the way it does every night. So for now, I will sit here relishing this last moment of quiet—except for the pounding upstairs—and let myself just be. In a minute, when I'm ready, I'll go be Mom.

Just Wait

ust wait. Since becoming a mother I've found myself bombarded with this phrase time and again.

"Right now, you want him to walk, but just wait until he does. Then, you'll be wishing he'd go back to sitting still."

"You get so excited for your kids to talk, but just wait. Soon, all you'll want is for them to shut up for thirty freakin' seconds."

"Sure, he loves his baby brother now, but just wait until the little one can take his toys. Then it's a whole different ballgame."

And on and on and on it goes.

I'm never quite sure how to respond when people throw this phrase at me. It's so alarmingly negative, so I-know-better-than-you that it always catches me off guard. Often, I can't pinpoint what kind of emotion the person imparting this bit of wisdom is hoping to elicit in me. Shame? Regret? Fear of the future? So many times, I've just given a half smile and said nothing at all.

Now that I've lived through these instances myself, I wish I hadn't let some of that negativity crowd out my enthusiasm for all the little firsts. I want to take my brand new mom-self by the shoulders and assure her that she's supposed to get excited about these milestones. I want to tell her there's no shame in being thrilled to the point of loud, obnoxious cheering the first time her son takes a wobbly step across the kitchen into her open arms. I want her to know that it's okay to simply appreciate the good in a moment instead of waiting around for the bad to show up.

Just wait, I'd tell her. When your son begins to talk it will be one of the most amazing transformations you'll have the privilege to witness in your life as a mother. He'll start off puzzling over sounds, tripping over a jumble of consonants and vowels, getting frustrated as you point to different objects while he urgently screams something that sounds like, "Sabook!" over and over. Then one day, a word you taught him will come tumbling out of his mouth and it will be gratifying in a way you could have never imagined.

Just wait. The day your son takes his first step will be the first day in a world of completely new possibilities. You will finally be able to take him to the playground and watch him climb the stairs to the jungle gym he's always had to watch from a distance; you will get the chance to walk beside him and enjoy the simple pleasure of holding his hand. Sure, it will be a foray into mischievous (and sometimes heart-stopping) independence, but it will also be a gift to watch him strut and stumble his way into a world outside the security of your arms.

Just wait. Giving your son a sibling will be better than any coveted LEGO set or ride on tractor you could buy him. Yes, they will fight and take each other's toys and one of them might accidentally pee on the other in the bathtub, but their bond will be rock solid and they will each have a built in best friend to share in all their most important memories. Seeing your children's love for each other will easily become one of the greatest joys of your lifetime.

Just wait, I'd tell her. It only gets better from here.

Growing By Degrees

Directly to the left of the fireplace in our family room is a large expanse of empty wall space. The rest of the room is covered in pictures of various sizes: a collection from our wedding day, a few of Chase as a newborn, one of our family of three at the beach. The empty space is conspicuous by comparison. We live in the house I grew up in after my parents moved away several years ago, so I know that spot well—it's the one where a large portrait of my mother on her wedding day hung for my entire life. It still has the nail there and everything.

We have lived in this house for over a year and have yet to fill that space with a picture, though I've thought about it many times. I found out I was pregnant with Sam shortly after moving in and I knew a portrait of our family of three would have to be replaced when our fourth member joined us. After Sam was born, I thought of using the only decent picture I have of the four of us together, but he was still a newborn when it was taken. He is now four months old, constantly changing. Staring at that empty space as I have so many times, I realized that any picture I put there would be instantly outdated. My boys are growing faster than I can document their lives. The realization is sobering, startling; when you're deep in the trenches of new motherhood, it can feel like it will all last forever. Of course, that's the furthest thing from the truth.

For the past two years, I have had the good fortune to be able to stay home with Chase and Sam, which is easily the best gift Adam has ever given me (except maybe my Kitchen Aid mixer, which ranks right at the top of the list). Every day I get to watch them grow a little at a time—learning new words they didn't know yesterday, developing new skills, physically maturing an inch or a pound at a time. I am there for it all, every last little detail.

But because that is true, I sometimes lose sight of the fact that they are growing and changing so rapidly. It seems it should be the opposite. Since I see them every day, the changes seem more gradual, more drawn out, and it gives me the illusion that I have more time with them at each stage than I actually do. Friends or family who see them less frequently are constantly remarking on how much they have grown, how their hair has changed color, how much steadier they are on their feet. I always smile and agree with them, but there have been many times where I just didn't see it. I've kept quiet because it makes me seem like an inattentive mother. How could I not notice that my boys are growing right before my eyes? How have I managed to miss the little things that are so plain to those who see them far less often?

I am aware that they are growing. I haven't buried my head so far in the sand that I've missed all of it. It's just that none of it seems as drastic when you spend every moment with your children, day after day. Or maybe it's that my yardstick for measuring their growth is different than the one that other people— even my husband—use. They track their development by more obvious markers: height, weight, physical and social abilities like walking and talking. For me, the signs are less tangible, more elusive. I don't always notice Sam's cheeks filling out or the new rolls that appear on his chubby legs, but then suddenly I am packing up another box of outgrown clothes and it stops me in my tracks: he will never be small enough to wear that onesie again. Between doctor's appointments I am often unaware of my Chase's changes in height, but then one day he is tall enough to turn the knob on the pantry door and get himself the granola bar he wants without my help. For many months I am in the habit of calling Sam a newborn, but then during a trip to the attic I notice the ExerSaucer in the corner and realize he is as old now as Chase was when he began using it.

For a short few weeks, Chase would answer "wert" when asked where daddy was on a weekday. It was an adorable mistake and I found myself going out of my way to keep from correcting him. My husband and I, who are often in the habit of conversing with each other in toddler-speak, would refer to his job as "wert," too. "How was wert today?" and "I'll be out of wert around 4:30." But then, one day, I noticed that Chase had learned how to say "work" correctly. Of course, I was proud that he figured it out all on his own, but part of me was heartbroken that "wert" had officially become a thing of the past. It was one tiny inconsequential syllable, but it felt momentous. It was like I'd witnessed a single frame in a time-lapse video of a caterpillar becoming a butterfly. That one second seems to mean nothing in the grand scheme of the whole transformation process, but when you see all those little seconds added together, it's indisputable proof that every moment matters.

These changes always sneak up on me when I fool myself into thinking a particular stage will last awhile. Suddenly they are onto something new and I am forced to adjust, though half of my heart is left behind in the old phase when they were still younger, still smaller, still further away from the day when they will no longer need me to help them pronounce a word correctly or reach the snack on the highest shelf.

The march of time in my world is steadier, less pronounced, but its subtlety makes it all the more heartbreaking; my children's years of being little are passing me by more quickly than I realize. Much of the time I am too caught up in the day-to-day routine to give it much attention. Then, in certain moments, I find myself faced with the irrefutable evidence of my children growing older. It is both exciting and tragic—I am caught in the gray area between celebrating all the firsts and mourning all the lasts.

I know I cannot stop time from marching forward, much as I want to keep my children little as long as possible. Soon enough, I will fill that empty spot on the wall with a picture of our family as we are now, a picture that will already be outdated the moment it is hung. By the time we wake up the next morning, our family will be different; maybe not in the noticeable ways, but in the subtle nuances only those with the benefit of a little distance can see. The baby's hair might be a slighter blonder tint than the day before or maybe the ghost of a wrinkle will have etched itself into my forehead overnight. Even if I really studied it, I might not be able to tell. But that picture on the wall will be tangible proof of how quickly time is passing; a reminder that, if I don't look closely, I'll miss the little things. Which, as it turns out, just so happen to be the big things.

The Us Before Them

You wake up in the dark of the morning and tiptoe to the shower while I am still asleep in our bed. The monitor perched on your nightstand emits the whoosh of the white noise setting on the boys' sound machines, each of them still asleep in their cribs down the hall. After your shower, you towel off, select your clothes in the half-darkness, do your best to keep the squeaky ironing board from jolting me awake. Usually, I hear it anyway—the closest thing I have to an alarm. Ear buds in, sports radio on, you iron your collared shirt and khakis, shave and brush your teeth, apply the cologne I got you two Valentine's Days ago when there were no kids down the hall yet and there was still time for each other. You bend to kiss me goodbye, reluctantly, heavily, as if there is nothing you want to do less than leave us. I know that's the truth. You don't hate your job; far from it. Sure, you complain like everyone does about work—someone broke the copier and didn't fess up, the new guy is always replying all on every email—but I know you enjoy what you do. Still, we are here and you are there and it's hard to be the one who is always gone.

During the day, I text you pictures of Chase scaling the big slide at the playground and Sam smiling wide-eyed into the camera wearing a new outfit he suddenly fits into. I want you to know that we are thinking of you, even though it feels like you are impossibly far, sitting in an office I've never seen because security clearances won't allow it. I want to picture you there and I try from what you've described to me, but the image never comes together. I realize I know so little about how you spend those 45 hours each week, the hours you spend longing to be here instead. "I miss my family," you text back nearly every time. "I wish I was home with you guys." We wish that too, I tell you, but we both know this is how it has to go; you are the more educated of the two of us, the one who has career aspirations and a solid path ironed out, whereas I left nothing behind but a too-small paycheck that would barely cover the cost of daycare.

I get lonely sometimes and I call so I can hear your voice, but you're in a meeting and when you call back I am in the middle of refereeing lunchtime. "Sorry I missed you," one of us says, and the other replies, "It's OK, just call when you're free." But then it's naptime and I can't talk because the baby always sleeps next to me while I work and I can't risk waking him. You have another meeting anyway, so we'll just talk on your way home.

My cell phone lights up with your picture as you leave the office and that call starts the 35-minute-long countdown until you arrive home, unless there's traffic or you have to stop off for the chicken I forgot was in the chicken and broccoli casserole I'm making as we speak. "Can we just talk when you get home?" I ask, because Chase is standing on the coffee table and Sam needs to be nursed. "Sure, I'll see you in 20 minutes." I note the time, hoping it'll be more like 18 or 19. Then you walk in the house and we are tired and cranky, all in desperate need of your attention and help right this minute. The toddler wants you to get him a snack that he just remembered he needs to eat immediately, the baby is tired of being ignored in the bouncy chair and I am hungrier, crankier and more exhausted than both of them combined. I retreat upstairs to "go to the bathroom," and get lost in doing something else entirely. I just want to be alone for five minutes, but sometimes it turns into ten or fifteen minutes and I hear you say, "Mama's coming back," but there's a question in your voice.

You've been home for a half hour and I suddenly realize you haven't even had the chance to change out of your work clothes, use the bathroom, crack a beer. You give over all your remaining stores of energy to us, your needy family, and by the time both boys are finally in bed for the night you're completely spent. So am I. There is nothing left for each other. Many nights I fall asleep before we pick a movie to watch on Netflix or you drift off alone downstairs on the couch while I peck away at my laptop, trying to get my fledgling writing career off the ground at the expense of our precious time together. I never meant for it to be like this, for us to become two ships passing in the night, for it to feel like sometimes we're living out different lives under the same roof. Before we had children, and later when we only had one, I pitied women who let their spouses become the last priority. You have to keep your marriage alive to raise children who know what real love looks like in practice, I thought (and, for the record, still do). I had no idea how hard it would be to make time for our marriage when each of us gives so much of ourselves to our children. How do we keep being good parents and keep being us, too? Is it possible? I desperately want to know it's possible.

The truth is, I miss us. I miss lazy Saturday mornings lying in bed wrapped up in each other, with nothing better to do than eat chocolate chip pancakes drowned in syrup before falling back asleep for hours. I miss our summer nighttime runs, learning the town where we owned our first house by exploring it on foot, racing each other down the straightaway of our street until we collapsed, breathless, on the front porch. I miss you coming home with a bottle of wine and saying, "Let's get drunk tonight," and actually being able to do that because all we had to worry about was sitting at a desk the next day and not waking up in the middle of the night with kids. I hate that it feels so hard to conjure up these memories because life has taken us so far from those times.

For us, the fortunate part is that we met each other early enough in life to get to spend more than a decade together before welcoming a baby into our family. But in some ways, that almost makes it harder. We had so long to get used to *us* that when Chase came along he signaled the end of our era of coupledom. I remember those early weeks when he wouldn't sleep without one of us holding him and we slept in shifts, one of us manning the baby while the other got a couple hours of fitful, inadequate sleep. Where just a few weeks before we spooned and cuddled at night, now we couldn't even sleep in the same bed together. I felt like I was losing you to our son and it scared the shit out of me.

It's possible that I've taken to romanticizing those memories in the years since. It is not to say that our time together wasn't as beautiful and wonderful as I thought, but I know that we spent much of those years dreaming of and planning for the incredible life that we have now, a life that I wouldn't trade for anything. Lying in bed on those Saturday mornings, we'd talk about the babies that would come someday, about what their names would be and whose eyesight they'd inherit, whether we'd celebrate Christmas with my family or yours, how we'd make sure they learned to ski much earlier than I did as a kid. The life that felt so far off in those days is here, and it's more than we ever could have dreamt of back then. It's still the end of an us as we knew it— the younger, more carefree us with unlimited time to spend loving each other—and, though I love the life we've created together as parents, I still sometimes mourn the couple we've left behind.

Will The Real Adult Please Stand Up?

I fumble around in the darkness, trying to locate the light switch in the pitch black of the master bathroom. I can't risk the light waking the baby, who is finally, blessedly asleep in the bassinet next to our bed, so I stand in total blackness until the door is closed and it's safe to flip the switch. The room suddenly floods with harsh fluorescent light. Through unfocused eyes, I catch a glimpse of myself in the vanity mirror—hair wild, complexion dull, wearing my husband's oversized, decade-old beer league kickball shirt, holey and frayed along the hem.

There is something strangely familiar there in the reflection; a mental image of my mom surfaces, wearing my father's oversized tee shirts to bed every night as far back as I can remember. In that moment—adorned in the same ridiculous sleepwear as my mother, the consummate picture of adulthood—I realize that, without even really noticing, I have somehow slipped into adulthood myself.

I am convinced that can't be true, though the signs are certainly all there. Within the relatively short span of 18 months I've given birth twice over. I've bestowed names upon those children, fed them from my body, changed several thousand diapers, caught puke in my hands. I taught myself how to make a chicken potpie from scratch and learned the hard way how to change a flat tire. There's a little boy in my bed who calls me "mama."

Yet there is always a reason to feel like an imposter. *I return library books late. We sometimes eat Cinnamon Toast Crunch for dinner. I do my taxes at the last possible minute every year and only pretend to know what most of the financial terms mean.*

I've spent years believing I still have time to become the kind of adult I thought my mother was during my childhood. Until now, I had never once stopped to consider that maybe she started out feeling exactly like I do at this moment.

She was 28 when she gave birth to me, her first baby, the same age I am now. Though I just assumed she fell into adulthood easily, it stands to reason that my mother didn't have everything figured out the morning she started her first real job, the day she walked down the aisle, the minute the nurse placed me in her arms.

Maybe she forgot doctors' appointments and didn't know how to sew Halloween costumes.

Maybe her mother had to help her make the turkey the first year she hosted Thanksgiving.

Maybe, amidst her fears and frustrations, she sometimes felt more like a little kid playing house than a real adult.

Maybe she just pretended to know what she was doing until she actually did.

I often find myself sending up a silent prayer of thanks that my kids will have no recollection of the ways in which I've screwed up so far. There's got to be a reason why it happens like that: why children don't remember much of their early years when the majority of their parents' trial and error occurs. That must be true or none of us would ever take our parents seriously.

Maybe adulthood is more of a gradual thing than an all-at-once thing.

Maybe you never completely figure it all out—you just get better at pretending.

Maybe, in the beginning, our parents were just scared kids like us who were totally winging it and hoping like hell that no one noticed.

The past couple of years I've been fumbling in the dark, trying to find the elusive adult gene that I assumed must have skipped a generation and left me to fend for myself. When the answers weren't readily apparent, I held my breath through the hard parts, waiting for the real adult to show up and tell me what to do.

But maybe all that time she was already here, looking back at me from the mirror; the girl in the too-big tee shirt with the wild hair and tired eyes who feels like she's just going through the motions until someone else takes over. The real adult who, like so many mothers before her, already has the answers. She just doesn't know it yet.

Thankful

It was 10:00 on Thanksgiving night. I'd spent the better part of a week prepping my house for seventeen people to descend upon it, starving and ready to celebrate a holiday centered around the food I was responsible for making. The whole ordeal was an unbelievable amount of work and, consequently, a ton of pressure. I worried more than once about things going wrong. What if my perfectly planned cooking strategy was ruined by a family member who showed up with uncooked food that required my entire oven immediately before dinner? (That happened.) What if the store whose employees specifically told me I didn't need to pre-order their homemade gravy ran out the day before Thanksgiving? (That happened, too.) What if the person who brought the pies forgot to actually cook the frozen crusts before filling them? (Yup. Happened.) I'd busted my ass all week attending to every little detail of shopping, prepping, cooking and cleaning. By the time I finally got to sit down after everyone had left I was flat-out exhausted. I couldn't wait to flip up the recliner, lie back and cuddle up to my husband who was zoned out watching football with a beer in hand after putting the toddler to sleep.

No sooner had I gotten comfortable than the baby began fussing upstairs. Normally not too bothered by the sound of crying, I was immediately on edge. "I'm going to give him a few minutes," I said, tentatively settling into the couch. It had taken me nearly an hour to get him to sleep, so I wasn't keen on starting that process all over again. Over the next several minutes, his cries got louder and more intense; crying gave way to wailing, then wailing to full-blown howling. I'd learned to decipher his different cries; he'd now reached the level that meant he wasn't going to calm down again unless I fed him.

In that moment, I wanted nothing more than to sit there on that couch in my pajamas, doing absolutely nothing that involved a tiny person sucking on my nipples. The thought of trudging upstairs, trying to feed him while he repeatedly fell asleep in my arms, putting him in his crib only for him to wake up again and then repeating whole charade at least five times over was unappealing to the point of being laughable. Except that instead of laughing, I just sat there and let my eyes fill with tears. The whole day I'd catered to everyone else's needs and just when I was finally about to sit down and devour a slice of pumpkin pie topped with a generous helping of whipped cream, the baby needed me. Not me, his mother, but me, the milk machine—the only person who could provide exactly what he needed at that moment.

As I plucked him out of his crib and settled into the rocker, I felt a sudden surge of anger at this tiny person who needed me so intensely at seemingly every important moment of every day. The moment I needed to be mashing potatoes in order to keep to my carefully-planned cooking schedule: he was hungry. The moment I'd specifically reserved for getting dressed before the guests arrived: he was hungry. The exact moment I sat down to eat the Thanksgiving meal I'd spent four days preparing: he was hungry. Being on-call 24 hours a day had finally gotten to me; I was burnt out and fed up. Sitting there in the dark with my little boy cradled close to my body, I wanted to feel gratitude for the gift of being able to breastfeed. Instead, I just felt fed up with all of it.

When I get to this point—as I do every so often—I always feel immense guilt. I struggled to breastfeed Chase and I fervently wished every day that I could nurse like so many other moms I knew. It made me feel inadequate and inept as a mother not to be able to feed my baby the way my body was designed to do. Now that I am successfully breastfeeding Sam, I feel guilty wishing I didn't have to some days. It's a gift to have a second chance but breastfeeding a child is so much more work than I anticipated. The first time around I was in a lot of pain, so that was what I'd prepared to deal with when I had my second baby. Until then, no one had told me the invaluable truth: "If it hurts, something is wrong." I believed something was wrong with *me*. Despite having delivered a baby without medication, I figured I must have a lower pain threshold than everyone else.

During my second pregnancy I prepared myself mentally to fight through the pain in order to breastfeed successfully. But as it turns out, when you're doing it right, it truly doesn't hurt; I had prepared for all the wrong things. What I didn't prepare for was the physical demand and the emotional sacrifice breastfeeding would require. I had very little idea of what it actually entailed outside of the correct positioning, the best nursing pillow, the perfect latch. I didn't know that it's constant planning and predicting. It's being needed non-stop without reprieve and being the only one who can stop the middle-of-the-night cries. It's pumping for three days so you can leave the baby for three hours. It's finally being out of the house alone and your boobs leaking through the shirt you just bought for the occasion. It's learning to become comfortable nursing your baby while you sit across from your Uncle Ed at Thanksgiving dinner and you both pretend like a tiny person isn't sucking on your breast while you eat your candied yams. I didn't know about any of it.

I'm intensely grateful most days for the gift of being able to breastfeed Sam. It has given me a bond with him that feels so much different than the one I had with Chase; we are connected in a way that defies explanation. Watching him grow and knowing it's a result of the nourishment I produced with my own body? Absolutely amazing. Without sounding like an informational video (Adam and I snuck out of our first and only breastfeeding class during a bathroom break because the video they showed was so over-the-top) feeding my baby from my body is nothing short of miraculous. But does it suck sometimes? Without a doubt. Knowing that ahead of time wouldn't have changed my decision to try again, but it certainly would have helped to prepare myself mentally for all that it would require of me.

Breastfeeding is an experience I desperately wanted when I couldn't have it but that I didn't fully understand until I did. I thought the hardest part was not being able to do it successfully; I had no idea that it would often feel just as frustrating when everything was going right. Now, when I think of it being over, it fills me with equal parts relief and devastation. I want the bond, but not the bondage; the sweet, but not the bitter. I know it doesn't really work that way, though. I don't get to pick and choose what parts I want to keep and do away with the rest.

Next Thanksgiving, there's a good chance that our breast-feeding journey will have come to an end. I'll be able to mash the potatoes without worrying about anyone's schedule but my own and, most likely, I'll get to enjoy my end-of-the-night pie in peace. Sam's dinner will be eaten from his highchair tray and my only role in feeding him will be to cut his turkey into bite sized pieces. Part of me will be thankful that everything will be that much easier, less complicated. Removing the obligation of breastfeeding will make the day run so much smoother. But a part of me will mourn the loss, even with the added complications it invited. When the chaos of the day reaches a fever pitch, I will wish I still had an excuse to sneak away to a quiet room to give my little boy that which only I can give him. Even though I sometimes wish it away, when it's finally over, I will miss this frustrating, all consuming, overwhelmingly beautiful bond that's uniquely ours.

Harder, Not Worse

*I*t's the Sunday after Thanksgiving and we're setting up our Christmas tree, as is our annual tradition. It's the first year that Chase will have any understanding of the holiday, though he's still too young to grasp the concept of driving to a field in the backwoods and cutting down a live tree, strapping it to the roof of our car, dragging it into the middle of our living room and hanging shiny things all over it. (For the record, I still don't quite grasp the concept myself.) After digging out the box of ornaments from the depths of our overcrowded attic, I select a plastic candy cane and attempt to teach Chase how to hang it on the tree. He watches intently while I show him, then grabs it from my hand to try himself. He lays the ornament on top of the branch, where it sits for half a second before falling to the floor. "Oops. Fall down," he says, then skitters back to the box to select a second one to hang. Before I can get there, he nabs a glass ornament from the box, which falls from his hand and shatters as it hits the floor. "Oh no!" he exclaims as my husband rushes to locate the broom and dustpan. For the duration of the tree trimming, we stick to non-breakable ornaments—plastic snowflakes, a hand sewn Christmas tree, sparkly icicles and glittery pinecones. Each one is piled in the same spot on the tree, then inevitably tumbles through the branches to the floor below. As each falls, he sets to work placing them back on the tree, determined to get them to stay the way the others we've hung above him do.

To look in on this scene, a childless person would think decorating a Christmas tree with kids has got to be about as enjoyable as a root canal or a trip to the DMV. There's a lot of extra work that goes into the process; the kinds of things you don't really think much about when you're free to place your non-breakable ornaments wherever you damn well please and you don't give a second thought to the possibility of your entire tree winding up toppled on the floor. Of course, it's not just limited to Christmas tree decorating—adding kids to pretty much any equation automatically multiplies the exhaustion factor by ten and the difficulty factor by twenty. I doubt many parents would argue with that. The problem is that I often find myself equating "harder" with "worse," even though that's not quite the truth.

I guess it makes sense why I think that way: everywhere I look, someone is offering a fix, a hack, a solution to make life easier. Trust me—I'm certainly not above that stuff and I have the Pinterest boards to prove it. Just like everyone else, I want to find the magic bullet that will ease my burdens and free up my time.

My kids are so much work. Some days it takes every last shred of patience and every remaining ounce of will I have just to get to bedtime without snapping. There are days when I don't make it that long and instead I yell and they cry and then I feel like a terrible mother who is irreparably screwing up her children. But thirty seconds later, one of them gives me a kiss for no reason at all and the equation balances itself, my infraction all but forgotten in their endlessly forgiving minds. I know these early years are a chance to work out some of the kinks while their memory still refreshes every three minutes like that of a goldfish. Someday they will be old enough to hold my mistakes and missteps against me for far longer. I'd be fooling myself if I believed that things automatically get easier as the kids get older, even though pretending that's true is sometimes the only thing that gets me through a particularly rough day.

It won't always be this hard, I tell myself while I'm up at 3:30 a.m. negotiating with a toddler who thinks it's time to be awake for the day. *Someday, all of this madness and chaos will be behind me and everything will be easier.* Just the other day I was with a friend in the children's room at the public library. Between the two of us we had five kids running around screaming and throwing books on the floor. Sitting at a table a few feet away were two girls, probably around ten or eleven, quietly reading chapter books to themselves while our children's chaos swirled around them. My friend nudged me and laughed, pointing out the girls. "Someday, right?" she said wistfully. I sighed back and smiled. "Someday." In that moment, being the mother of those girls looked easier than being the mother to a gaggle of wild animals closely resembling small children in Baby Gap outfits. But maybe the mother of those girls was looking at us and remembering how much easier it used to be when she didn't have to worry about her girls wanting iPhones or creating Instagram accounts behind her back. Maybe the mothers of teenagers long for the years I am in now when everything isn't a battle worthy of slammed doors and rolled eyes. Maybe the mothers of grown children wish to be back right in this messy, chaotic phase when their kids were still solely theirs and they didn't have to share them with the world. Someone else's life always looks a little easier from the outside. I don't think any mother's circumstances are ever truly easy; they're just different.

Something tells me that motherhood isn't supposed to be one of those "easier is better" things, like efficiently storing wrapping paper or making mess-free pancakes. The reward lies in the difficulty of it all; of putting in the work to sew the seeds and then having the good fortune to watch them bloom and thrive. To me, the harder is more enjoyable, at least most of the time. Yes, it takes infinitely longer when my son helps me vacuum than when I do it alone, but it's also not nearly as much fun; I love to watch how excited he gets when I let him help. Of course, grocery shopping takes, on average, double the time and triple the effort with my kids in tow, but I secretly love how eager other people in the store are to interact with them. And, undoubtedly, trimming a Christmas tree with a toddler is a lesson in patience, but one I wouldn't trade for all the symmetrically decorated trees in the world, glass ornaments be damned.

Body on Loan

From the moment I got pregnant with my first child, I started the gradual process of giving my body away one touch at a time. If asked, I couldn't even begin to estimate how many times a day I'm touched. Hundreds? Thousands? Maybe, more accurately, my day is just one continuous touch from the moment I wake up with my son's 98th-percentile head crowding my pillow to the moment I fall asleep with my husband's arms cocooning my midsection. It's a strange dynamic that no one seems to talk about during pregnancy: how your body can go from being solely yours to being on loan to everyone in your family who seems to need it more.

When you think about it, it's funny how you're sort of eased into the whole thing. Instead of starting with the swollen ankles and huge protruding belly right off the bat, you begin with the mostly unnoticeable signs: the nausea, the fatigue, the heightened sense of smell. The fact that gestation takes so long affords you time to get used to the concept of sharing your personal space with someone else; this little being who starts as no more than a tiny collection of cells and nine months later is a fully-formed, watermelon-sized person whose left foot is constantly lodged under your ribcage. When I was pregnant with Chase, I celebrated the changes in my body with the appropriate amount of awe and wonderment knowing that, while it seemed to last forever, it was but a brief moment of sharing my body. Especially after the unfathomable heartache of my miscarriage, I appreciated that pregnancy is a gift and I didn't want to waste it being miserable. What I didn't realize then was that the sharing of my body would not end when my child was born. In actuality, it was just beginning.

After giving birth, I surrendered so much more of my body to my baby than I ever did during pregnancy. Chase didn't sleep without someone—usually me—holding him for the first six weeks of his life. Since I was too afraid to put him in bed with us, most nights I slept on the couch with him propped up on my chest, his tiny body covering me from neck to waist. As he wriggled and squirmed throughout the impossibly long night, I couldn't help but notice the similarity to all those nights he'd kept me awake during my pregnancy, jabbing and kicking from the inside. Only this time, I didn't see an end in sight. It quickly became clear—even after Chase learned to sleep on his own—that my days of bodily autonomy were long gone. Unable to breast-feed, I also became a round-the-clock slave to the breast pump; no sooner would I finish than I'd have to wash the parts and start all over again. I'd watch my nipples being stretched to their absolute limit while the mechanical drone of the pump assault-ed my senses and wonder how I'd become this person in such a short amount of time. Between pumping, rocking, holding, changing, wearing, feeding and bathing with my baby, I found myself being touched nearly every minute of every day. Most days I didn't really mind it, and others I truly savored it. But there were many days when giving up not only my identity, but also my entire body felt like too big a sacrifice to have to make, even for my own child. What was left that was just mine?

I didn't truly understand what it meant to be "touched out" until I gave birth to Sam, however. Chase was a very independent little person from the start; he preferred his own company and was always content entertaining himself, whether batting at the dangling toys on his play mat as an infant or coloring a picture alone at the table as a toddler. Even as a young baby he'd turn his head at kisses and resist snuggles with every iota of his being. In fact, his first word was "down," as in "put me down." There were many times I begged for his affection only for him to wriggle and squirm his way out of my reach.

My second son could not be more different—he prefers to be held all day long and craves constant interaction. Sam smiled—really smiled, not those gassy reflexes—at only four weeks old, a born flirt. He loves to be touched: held in our arms, bounced on our knees, snuggled up against my chest while nursing, kept close in the front pack. I've seen Chase literally lay down on top of him or climb right into his car seat with him and all Sam does is smile back. As long as he's being touched, he's happy.

Which, of course, means that he and I are attached almost constantly. If he's not nursing, he's in the front pack while I unload dishes or make breakfast; I sit him in my lap while Chase and I play on the floor and I have worn him on my body while I go to the bathroom more times than I can count on two hands (or feet). Since his brother was born, Chase has wanted to get in on the action too. He will sit so close to me that the whole side of his body—from shoulder to foot—is pressed right up against mine without a centimeter of space between. Now, if he's draped over a hip while I make dinner or snuggled up with me on the couch before bed, his fingers are absentmindedly stroking my arm or patting my leg. If I'm in the bathroom, he is constantly trying to pry my thighs apart to see what's happening; if we're in the shower, he's quizzically poking and prodding my various body parts. In their needier moments, it feels like every time they touch me, my kids come away with a little bit of me on their always-sticky hands—almost like they're siphoning from my tank to fill up their own. By the end of the day, they are bouncing off walls and careening around corners, their tanks full to capacity with every drop of love and selflessness I have to spare; and I am barely chugging along, my tank depleted, bone dry.

Most of the time I revel in their proximity. They are boys, after all, and I know they won't tolerate my affection forever. Truly, some of my happiest moments are when both of them are crowded right on top of me and I get the chance to pepper their heads with kisses and whisper how much I love them in their tiny ears. In those moments, I am hyperaware of the cautionary murmurings of older, wiser mothers who have told me to cherish it because it won't last. Most of the time I do. But sometimes the thought of being touched by one more person makes me want to jump out of my skin.

Unfortunately, that one more person is usually my husband. My adoring, sweet, loving husband who spends all day staring at a computer screen and wishing he was home with his family. My warm, demonstrative husband whose touch I absolutely cannot stand when my own sensory tolerance is on overload. It gives me endless guilt to feel that way. We have always been one of those obnoxiously affectionate couples that constantly need to be touching in some way; a hand on a leg, an arm around a shoulder, holding hands when we walk through the grocery store, standing in the kitchen hugging for long minutes for no reason at all. It used to make me laugh that he never wanted to sit across from me in a restaurant if it was just the two of us and, despite the waitress' dirty looks, would move to my side of the table simply so we could share more oxygen. We started dating in high school as hormonal teenagers so touching was kind of our thing, but now we have children who have claimed my body for their own and there is little left for him at the end of some days. At the moment he walks through the door, he craves intimacy and touch and I crave solitude and personal space. Sometimes, the chasm between our respective wants and needs feels impossibly wide.

More often than not, I just need time to regroup at the end of the day. After we put the kids to bed, I take my place on the opposite end of the couch, truly requiring that foot of space between me and any other living thing. As the night goes on, I find myself reaching across the divide to hold Adam's hand or inching closer to snuggle up beside him. By the time we retire to our bed, I'm usually content to be spooned or, at the very least, have one limb or another touching his beneath the sheets. And then there are nights when the kids have been in bed for hours and I still cannot bear to be so much as grazed in passing.

Still, I know that I am one of the lucky ones; not every woman is fortunate enough to be so loved that people literally want to hang all over her body twenty four hours a day. My family's love is manifested in touch; in the physical ways in which they show me how much they need me. If I ever lose sight of how much I am loved, I can just look to the hands around my legs or the head buried in my neck and remember that their affection is a gift that I'm lucky enough to receive. Even when it is stifling and I'm nearing critical mass, I cannot lose sight of the fact that it won't last forever. And when this period of constant body sharing finally ends, I'll be begging them to give me just one more touch.

In the meantime, I need just an inch of breathing room, an iota of personal space. I'm not asking for complete bodily autonomy—I know that's not realistic in this season of my life—just when it gets to be too much to take. Though I truly love and appreciate their grasp on my heart, sometimes I wish everyone around me would just keep their hands to themselves.

Mother, In the Possessive

When Adam and I were first married, there was a particular rush I associated with uttering the phrase "my husband." It was a stamp of ownership—a claim to something outside of myself. "This person chose to spend the rest of his life with me," the phrase implied. "I belong to someone and he belongs to me." The symbol of my attachment flashed on my fourth finger as a warning sign to singles trolling in bars, an emblem of solidarity to other pairs browsing aisles of complicated Swedish handiwork at IKEA.

Then I became a mother and the entire lexicon of words in the possessive form grew. Suddenly, every other word had an apostrophe attached: "my baby's chubby feet," or "my toddler's habit of picking his nose at the dinner table." It was a rush far superior to that of marriage and partnership: it's the mark of someone who physically created another human being, who willed them into existence with an ovulation chart, a cycle of

IVF, or a night of tequila shooters that ended in a little blue plus sign and nine months of a perma-hangover.

It was a momentous feeling to speak those words for the first time. About two days after Chase was born, I overheard Adam telling a nurse at the hospital about Chase's breastfeeding habits. "Our son is always doing this thing where he pops off after latching," my husband explained, like it was the habit of a lifetime much longer than 48 hours. It was adorably catching; I found myself going out of my way to expound on *my son's* features and qualities, to offhandedly inform perfect strangers in line at Starbucks that I was a mother, the authority on exactly one thing in the known world. I felt like the universe had given me a pat on the back: "You're really a mom now. Go ahead and help yourself to all the new possessives you'd like."

Then, Sam came along. When he did, there was an equally fulfilling thrill that accompanied the phrase, "my firstborn," or "my younger son," because it meant I was responsible for creating and nurturing more than one entire human life, even though I've never been able to keep a houseplant green for longer than two weeks.

I found myself talking about "my first pregnancy," and wearing it like a badge of honor because, if I had a first it's implied that I had a second or a third or a ninth. The possessives have begun to crop up more often in my vocabulary—I use them in mommy groups on Facebook when dispensing advice to someone struggling with sleep training, in the checkout line at the grocery store when I lock eyes with another mom trying to keep three kids from swiping chocolate off the lowest shelves, in the ER waiting room when I plead with the receptionist to please find someone to see my son.

My new symbol of ownership isn't a ring that cost three months' salary, but a diaper bag loaded with every conceivable item my sons might need in the next three months, an SUV full of Happy Meal debris, and a slightly stooped look from years of nursing, giving piggyback rides and racing matchbox cars on the floor. I spot another mom browsing the aisles of overpriced swaddle blankets at Babies "R" Us and even if she's not with her kids I know she's a mom, too—she's got the marks to prove it.

I'm relatively new to this expanded vocabulary, so perhaps I'll learn in time that the novelty wears off. Maybe the words become commonplace and dull from frequent use—it seems logical that they don't provide that same zing of excitement when you're on the receiving end of *my preschooler's* temper tantrum or *my teenager's* repeated eye rolls—but when I witness the way my parents' eyes still light up when they talk about me and my sister, I tend to think those little apostrophes are going to be with me for life. Still, you won't hear me complaining; my old vocabulary felt like it was missing something anyway.

It's OK That You Didn't Stay Home

Dear Mom,

Now that I have the good fortune of being a stay-at-home-mom, I can see you feel guilty that you couldn't stay home with me when I was little. When I ping your inbox with a picture of an aquarium trip or a picnic in the park at 1:30 p.m. on a Tuesday, I know you are reminded of something you consider your shortcoming as a mother. But I want to tell you something: it's OK that you didn't stay home.

Because you worked, you gave me a sense of ease with the unfamiliar that I may never have learned had you been by my side every moment of every day. You always loved to tell people about how well I adapted to new situations, about the fact that I would approach other kids at school and ask very directly if they wanted to be my friend.

I gained that boldness because you gave me the independence to find my own way in the world.

Because you worked, I learned about what work-life balance looked like in practice. No, you didn't let me milk an exaggerated illness to stay home from school or whisk me out of math class to go to the beach on a Friday, but you were there every single time I needed you to deliver a book report left on the kitchen counter or sit in the stands while I ran a 25-second race in a track meet that stretched across the better part of an afternoon. Just because you worked doesn't mean you missed out on my childhood; you were there in the foreground of all my most significant milestones, your job always less important than the things that were important to me.

Because you worked, my childhood is stocked with memories of ice cream cones on the boardwalk in Virginia Beach, outrageously priced G.A.P. sweatshirts I *had* to have to fit in at school, tickets to Matchbox 20 concerts and brand new L.L. Bean backpacks with pink embroidered monograms. Because you worked, I was able to attend the college of my dreams and will only be paying off my student loans for the next 30 years instead of the next 60. You should know that I often wrestle with my choice to be a stay-at-home-mom, knowing that I may not be able to afford to give my boys the life—and the memories—you gave me.

Because you worked, I was proud that you were my mom. I remember visiting you during the workday, following the colored lines on the hospital floor to the elevator and pushing the #3 for the Accounting wing. Your job seemed so significant to me; you with your very own office, with your own phone that you answered so importantly, expertly discussing cash flow and balance sheets and things I still don't understand. When I came to visit, you always reminded me that you were still a mom above all else, with snacks hidden in the bottom drawer of her filing cabinet.

Why do I want you to know this now, several decades and two grandchildren later? Maybe because becoming a mother myself has finally made me understand your side of things: the ever-present guilt you feel for each choice you make, always wondering if it's the wrong one, the one that will change your children's lives irrevocably. I want you to know that your choice did change my life, but not in the way you always feared. I am who I am *because* you worked, not in spite of it.

So thank you, Mom. I owe you one.

With gratitude,

Melissa

Outside Our Bubble

The world outside our four walls has become a terrifying reality. Though I am not always up to date on the latest news—or even last month's news, if I'm being honest—I don't have to look hard to find evidence of the world caving in on itself. It's splashed all over my News Feed, trumpeted across the headlines of the newspaper, the evils of this life all but seeping out of the screens and pages. While browsing Facebook's trending topics, it strikes me how much it reads like a debriefing of all that is wrong with the world: a mass shooting at a California elementary school, a baby abandoned in a Dumpster behind a New York City café, a teenager who committed suicide in the wake of relentless hazing.

I am not an alarmist, especially when it comes to my children. I don't gasp when they fall, I don't obsessively bathe all of us in hand sanitizer after we go to playgroup. They have to learn about the way life works by being full participants in it, even if it means they'll suffer some of the unfortunate consequences of being alive. I know that. I've steeled myself for the day when someone picks on them at the playground or the first time they truly fail at something that felt important to them. I have no doubt that it will hurt me even more than it hurts them, but I will take comfort in knowing it's all a part of growing up and into oneself.

But there is so much I'm just not prepared for; so much I'm not ready to expose them to yet (or, if I'm being honest, maybe ever). The bomb threat at the middle school. The foreign war that another mother's child is fighting. The cyberbully hiding behind an iPhone screen and the real life bully sitting at the next desk in Spanish class. It's enough to make me want to hide my children away, to keep them from experiencing life beyond our four walls if it means they will remain safe.

Right now they are so little and I still have some measure of control over their world. It won't last, but a mother can dream.

For the moment their entire world is primary colors and plastic trucks, Teddy Grahams and footed pajamas. They know only what I allow them to know of the world; the rest is just a question mark in their curious minds.

They are not aware that there are hardships beyond broken crayons or inequities greater than mommy eating the last bite of her own ice cream cone. The biggest injustice they will face today is not being permitted to watch a second episode of Curious George or having to stop playing because it's naptime.

The only battle they will fight this morning is with each other over who will get more of mommy's attention. For now, they know nothing of the evil and terror that exists down the street, in the neighboring town, across the globe. They are not scared of the world's ills because, for the moment, they don't have to concern themselves with any of it.

I wish I could let them go on like that forever, blissfully ignorant, safe and protected. I long to keep them in our little bubble where no one can harm them and they are immune to all the countless ways in which they will, undoubtedly, be hurt one day. I want them to sail through heartbreak, skate by illness, dodge loss and grief. Yet I know that's unrealistic—the world beckons them and one day I will no longer be able to keep them from answering. I'll be forced to put them on a school bus with a driver I've never met, watch their little faces disappear from view and trust that they will be alright without my protection.

For a time, they will come back to me at the end of each day. I will still get to have some jurisdiction over their afternoon snacks, the amount of television they're allowed to watch before dinner, the number of bites of green vegetables they have to take before being excused from the table. For a bit longer, I will still be afforded the privilege of reading them bedtime stories, tucking them in at night and knowing that, even if they wake up ten times asking for water, they are still exactly where I expect them to be, safe under our roof. For the foreseeable future, when I send them off into the world I will know a good amount about how they spend their days—what they had for lunch, which books they're reading in class, how they did on their spelling tests.

Then, slowly, I will begin to lose the thread of control. It won't happen all at once—these things never do. In fact, they'll be so gradual I might not even notice at first. One day, when I ask Chase what he did at recess, he will brush me off with a vague answer that won't seem like a big deal at the time. *Must've just been a boring day*, I'll think. "Did your report card come home today?" I'll ask Sam who is always honest to a fault. "No, they must be late," he will respond and I won't know he's lying to me because he's on the verge of failing sixth grade science. "Who's going to be at Andrew's party?" I'll inquire when I notice Chase wearing the shirt I know is his favorite before I drop him off for the evening. "I don't know," he'll mumble and I'll have no idea that there will be girls there or that someone will want to play Seven Minutes in Heaven because he is old enough to attend a party without my supervision.

In this new life outside our bubble, I will only know what they allow me to know; they will now be the gatekeepers and I will be the one on the other side, peeking through the fence posts to catch a glimpse of the happenings inside. The roles will reverse in a way that feels unfairly abrupt, though it was a process that began from the moment they were born. I will know less and less of the world outside our bubble, until, eventually the bubble will burst completely and I will no longer be able to protect them at all.

I know this is a natural progression. I often have to remind myself that it's a blessing to watch my children grow older, to see them tick off milestones and celebrate birthdays, heartbreaking as they are at times. The real heartbreak would be never getting the chance to witness any of it because an illness or loss precluded those milestones. Though I am reluctant to watch them outgrow me, it is a privilege not all parents are afforded.

Someday many years from now, I will stand at the end of the driveway as my son's car—a shiny new SUV that he bought with the paycheck from his first real job—will back onto the street and slowly disappear from my view. His girlfriend will be sitting in the passenger seat—a girl I like enough, but would never choose for him myself—and he'll navigate back to his own bubble, slowly retreating from the place where I have, momentarily, been able to keep him safe again. A part of me will leave with him; a little piece of my heart tucked in with his faded jeans and dress socks, wedged between his designer toiletry case—a gift from his girlfriend—and his old beat up running sneakers.

Someday, I will know so little about how he spends his days except what he tells me in hurried five-minute conversations between work and the gym. I won't know that his boss is an asshole or that his landlord raised the rent, that he finally learned how to cook risotto without burning it. I will know only the bits and pieces of his life that he deems necessary for me to know and I will not be able to keep him safe from the heartache and injustice in his life that he's told me nothing about. Someday, I will hold my sons' babies in my arms and remember what it was like when I was still my boys' whole world, the only existence of which they were aware.

Today they are still little. Our life together is the only life they know and I can still keep them safe from all that lies beyond our front door. Someday they will leave our bubble—leave me—to become the men I've raised them to be and live in a world from which I'll no longer be able to protect them. But today I am grateful. Because today is not that day.

The Reluctant Understudy

My first kid was easy. Like slept-through-the-night-at-eight-weeks easy. Like plays-by-himself-with-no-problem easy. He puked his way through the whole first year and never quite got the hang of breastfeeding, but, overall, I didn't have much to complain about when it came to being his mom. "You guys don't even really know what it's like to be parents," my mother-in-law said one day when she was returning him from an overnight at her house. Which probably sounds a little bit snotty to an outsider, but I got what she meant. Chase is well-behaved. He's independent. He's smart and freakin' hilarious. She was right—I didn't really know. In many ways it was like I was auditioning for the lead role of "Mom" with Chase, when, in reality, I was just the understudy learning the ropes and chewing her nails behind the curtain.

Then Sam was born and I found myself being thrust onto the stage, under the hot spotlight where every imperfection became uncomfortably pronounced. (Hey there, adult acne!) I thought I knew the lines by heart but, with so much at stake, they all evaporated from my mind. It quickly became clear that I was not as prepared as I'd thought. Let the ad-libbing commence.

If I'd had a camera crew follow me around for the first several months of being a mom to two kids under a year and a half, there would've been some seriously damning footage in there. I had no idea what I was doing, which is why it's fortunate my kids a) aren't verbal enough to divulge my secrets, and b) are too young to remember any of it for more than a quarter of an episode of Peppa Pig. My early ineptitudes are safely locked in the vault of my children's underdeveloped memories, where they will forever stay, lest a therapist coaxes them out sometime in their mid-30s when Sam has a flashback about being fed a dime by his two-year-old brother.

There was a lot I didn't know but I took comfort in the fact that they weren't things I could've prepared for ahead of time; it was all on-the-job training. For instance, getting both my kids downstairs every morning. Sounds simple, right? I'd be sitting in my room, folding a basket of laundry or playing on Facebook, when I'd hear one of them start stirring on the monitor. Inevitably, the other one would chime in mere seconds later. It was like they were somehow sending each other signals through the walls of their adjoining rooms—*I think mom is actually sitting down right now. Let's make sure that doesn't happen again for the next eight hours.*

"I guess we're just jumping right in," I'd think and then try to figure out which one to tackle first. The infant would be howling, causing my boobs to leak through the front of my crusty camisole, but the toddler was much more impatient and knew if he yelled "mama" eighty five times in a row, I'd probably choose him first. Which I usually did. *Well played, Chase.* I'd go in to get him up and he'd want to show me the bird on the neighbor's front lawn or the sock that fell behind the crib, all while the baby's screaming had reached the hiccupping/wheezing/silent screaming phase and we're in there chatting about the "doggy" across the street that is, in fact, actually a garbage can. Then I'd convince Chase to leave his crib with promises of milk and we'd go in to get Sam who had decided to stop screaming because clearly no one was listening. Chase would want to get in the crib with his little brother, so I'd oblige and lift him over the edge where he'd promptly kick Sam in the face. Now everyone would be crying, the whole place would smell like stale urine and we'd still have yet to move any closer to the stairs.

Ten minutes later we'd finally get to the top and I'd realize, *how the hell am I going to get them both down there?* Chase walks, but going down 14 stairs with him is the equivalent of following behind an arthritic octogenarian during a 5K. In a word: glacial. So I'd do the only reasonable thing: tuck one kid under each arm wide receiver-style and hustle down the stairs while both of them wailed their disapproval. After deciding how to feed them both simultaneously (one from my body and one from my fridge), getting each of them into clean diapers and firing up Netflix, I'd be absolutely exhausted. And it would be 7:34 a.m.

Later on we might decide to try leaving the house, which would be very ambitious and also unreasonably optimistic. Of course, we'd all still be wearing pajamas so we'd have to tackle real clothing first. The concept of wearing clean clothes is a good one, but the wheels would fall off the operation because, of course, there would be six piles of dirty laundry and the stuff I thought I put into the dryer yesterday would still be in the washing machine marinating in stagnant water considering I left the lid open again. A pair of backup shorts with weird seams and a sauce-stained tee shirt from the pile would have to suffice. Then we'd have to stop to discuss something urgent that I cannot decipher and also to locate the toddler's left shoe, which would tack approximately 63 minutes onto our departure time. (The shoe was in the crockpot. Obviously.)

Before Sam was born, leaving the house with a toddler had become old hat. We didn't need much except diapers, wipes and endless amounts of snacks, because anything we were missing could be successfully supplemented with Goldfish or Teddy Grahams. But getting out with a newborn AND a toddler is something akin to being a contestant on Supermarket Sweep—everyone is careening through the aisles tossing things in the diaper bag while the peanut gallery is counting down to the play date that started five minutes ago. Pacifiers and burp cloths, bibs and blankets, wipes, a hat and the entire contents of the bottom dresser drawer just in case of an incident involving bodily functions. And there's always something crucial you forgot, like, oh yeah, THE DIAPERS. (Which obviously happened to me at Sam's very first doctor's appointment and he had to wear his brother's size-four diaper home. Whoops.)

Like I said, I had a lot to learn. But then something really great happened: in time, I finally memorized my lines. Not without some mistakes—Chase recently fell out of his booster seat when I let go of his hand so I could reposition the baby—but, in general, I've got the hang of the logistics. Actually raising two kids though? That's a whole different story.

Second Born

*I*f you were to walk through our house on any given day, you would be confronted with evidence of Chase everywhere. His finger paintings fill up the corkboard in the playroom, his Matchbox cars are, puzzlingly, in the bathroom vanity, his grinning mugshot hangs above the mantel with the rest of his life's memories splashed across the walls in 5x7 frames. He is knitted into the very fabric of our home—the sounds, the smells, the crayon doodles on the walls and the teeth marks on the crib—his noise echoing through the hallways, his presence bursting from the rooms and spilling out the doors.

And then there is Sam, the second-born. From the very beginning, we knew he would be our more easygoing baby. His birth was absent the chaotic fanfare of Chase's arrival and breastfeeding went off without a hitch. The second week of his life, he contentedly slept through a multi-hour newborn photography session as I exploited his cuteness by placing him in wicker baskets and adorning him with colored scarves. (Sorry about that, by the way.) (But not that sorry.)

He is smaller and quieter, easier to overlook than his older brother, the food-covered blur that crashes and careens through the house. He is good-natured and not prone to tantrums. Except when he's hungry, he commands much less attention than his brother who is perpetually talking, crying, jumping, sprinting and devouring all in the same breath. He is the less-squeaky wheel, the lamb to Chase's lion, a tiny pinging triangle to his brother's brassy, blaring trumpet.

When I was pregnant with Sam I felt constant, unrelenting guilt that Chase would be pushed to the backburner upon the arrival of his baby brother. I envisioned all these heartbreaking scenarios in which I would be nursing the baby or changing his diaper and Chase would be crying for his mama to pay attention to him. The whole idea of it twisted my stomach with guilt. Then Sam was born and I realized how laughable my expectations were. It's not Chase who waits; it's Sam, always Sam. Sam waits for me to nurse him because his brother has to be buckled into his booster seat first. Sam waits for me to change his diaper because his brother's toy car is stuck behind the couch. Sam waits for me to collect him from his crib or the bouncy seat or the foot of the bed because his brother's shoe feels weird or he ate something out of the garbage. At first I felt guilty about that too, but now I realize it's just the way it works with the second born. They grow more and more patient as they learn that they will almost always have to wait for what they want. Most of the time I figure I'm helping build his character. Sometimes I just feel like I'm failing at being a mother to two young kids.

One morning several months ago, the boys and I were hanging out in the playroom when it became clear that I needed to change

Chase's diaper immediately. Without even considering Sam, I hauled Chase onto the changing table across the room and got to work cleaning him up. Moments later, I looked over and realized I'd accidentally left Sam sitting by himself; since he was new to sitting on his own and wasn't quite stable enough to leave for several minutes, I'd been in the habit of laying him down whenever I needed to do something that required me to leave his immediate vicinity. Sure enough, with both hands occupied and a snowball's chance in hell of abandoning my poop-covered oldest on the changing table, I watched as Sam fell face-first onto the playroom floor. It felt like it happened in slow motion while I looked on, completely helpless to intervene. Stranded on his belly and wailing in distress, Sam had to wait for me to finish with his brother before I could comfort him. But by the time I was finished wiping, re-diapering and putting Chase's pants back on, Sam had rolled to his side, no longer crying. I felt a surge of overwhelming guilt. I'd not only neglected to think of my second born entirely but couldn't even provide the comfort he needed when my split-second decision caused him to get hurt. To make matters worse, after being ignored for so long, he'd simply given up. Though it was a relatively small moment in the history of being a mother to two children, it's still one of several occasions that sticks out in my mind as being particularly guilt-inducing.

When Chase began potty training, my guilt ratcheted up even more. The spotlight had always shown more brightly on him and now I was forced to make him the true star of the show as I hurried him back and forth to the potty and followed him around with a spray bottle and a roll of paper towels for most of the day. Through it all, Sam just waited patiently, almost as if to say, "I know you can't handle both of us right now, Mom." At the end of the second night of potty training, Adam looked across the playroom at Sam sitting by himself with all his toys out of reach while we both helped Chase on the potty and remarked, "When Chase goes off to college, mommy and daddy will pay attention to you again, Sammy." I laughed, but my heart ached at the truth in his statement.

I often worry that Sam's first word will be "holdonSam," which I find myself saying on repeat nearly all day long. I know it's really no one's fault—just an unfortunate consequence of his place in the birth order—but it still doesn't seem quite fair. I want to have enough time for both of them. I want, in certain moments, to be able to divide myself in half. I want them each to feel important every moment of the day, regardless of which one has my immediate attention. But the reality is that the louder, bolder, needier one is usually the one who takes priority. The other one is simply made to wait.

Still, I will try like hell to convince my sweet, good-natured second born that even though he is quieter and takes up slightly less space than his brother, he is much more than just a footnote to Chase's story. I will make sure he knows that even though I have to look a little bit harder to find the evidence of him, he is surely there. He is in the curves of my body that was so recently his home. His name is constantly on his brother's lips—the first person Chase wants to see when he wakes up in the morning and the last person he kisses before bed. His heavenly baby scent is on every single piece of clothing I own, lingering there, defying washing machine cycles, fabric softener and dryer sheets. In such a short period of time, he has become firmly engrained in our family makeup, crucial to the chemistry of our kinship. Sam may not be the loud and commanding type (though it's very possible that will change with time), but he is a force all his own. He was not the first to join our family, but was the one who made it complete, at least for the foreseeable future. There is quite a lot to be said for that.

Survival Mode

Recently I was texting back and forth with a friend of mine who has three kids under three. She and I were pregnant with our youngest sons at the same time, so we'd often send the kinds of check in texts that first consisted of sentiments like, "I'm so uncomfortable, get this baby out of me," and now that both boys are here read more like, "I'm so tired, get these kids away from me." This latest time, I pinged her to ask how she and her family were doing.

"We are constantly in survival mode," she responded. "Which is fine, I guess, but I'd like to be past that."

"I know what you mean," I sympathized. "It's so much fun, but it's always something. No sleep or someone's sick or whatever the flavor of the day is."

"Yep. And you're right. It's usually fun and I do love it. I just want to enjoy it more. Is that bad?"

Even though we were both laughing as she described her daughter's latest habit of removing her diaper during the night and peeing all over her bed, I knew there was some gravity to our words. We are both in that messy, chaotic phase of beginning a family that is often rife with frustrations. In that phase it's not the big things that really get you—you learn to feed on demand and operate on minimal sleep pretty quickly—it's the little stuff, the misplaced shoes or the rolled eyes, that pushes you over the edge without warning. She had said out loud what I am always so afraid to admit: sometimes I don't enjoy motherhood so much as I survive it.

Of course, there are many moments, even whole days, when being a mother is so much damn fun. Overall, my kids are pretty happy little people and they give me cause to laugh nearly all day long. Even when Chase is getting in trouble for something, we both can't help but crack a smile most of the time. My life is richer and fuller now than it ever was before I had children. But if I said motherhood felt like that all the time, I'd be lying.

Some days—the ones where no one wakes up during the night and they both sleep past 5:30 a.m.—we wake up feeling ready to take on the morning. We snuggle on the couch and make break-fast, drive trucks and sing songs before we head out to a class or a play date. By the time we get back, they're ready for lunch and naps and then, before I know it, Adam is calling to say he's on his way home. The smiles are abundant and the mood is light; I'm not constantly yelling to stop eating that or stop hitting him and I feel like I have at least some of it together.

But then there are the days that start off on the wrong note and everything stays slightly off key for the duration; the ones that have me checking the clock all day, escaping into the solace of my phone, cursing under my breath or right out loud where Chase can mimic every word. The ones where all the little things pile up until they become big things: canceled plans and naptime meltdowns, uneaten lunches and husbands who work later than expected. And on those days, I feel like I'm not so much enjoying my kids as I am surviving them.

Then I wonder the same thing my friend contemplated in our recent conversation: *Is that bad?* Deep down in my bones I know it's not, but I'm still in the early phase of accepting that motherhood isn't quite like I imagined it would be before I had children. Maybe we all come into it with these grandiose ideas of what being a mother will look like but then have to shift our expectations once we're really living it.

I guess one of the things I expected was that, even when motherhood was hard—and I wasn't naïve enough to think it wouldn't be—I'd still enjoy all of it. I didn't envision having to work so hard to find the good in certain days, especially when things weren't really that bad on paper. If everyone is healthy, safe and relatively intact, I figured the day couldn't be that terrible; people clearly just didn't know what to expect from motherhood, so they let themselves get caught up in the negative. Then I found out how misleading the notion of "enjoy every minute" really is.

"I'm trying really, really hard to enjoy the little moments," my friend later said, "but it's very hard to do when my 3-year-old has taken off her diaper during the night and not put it back on, therefore causing her to wet the bed in a serious way for several days in a row." I read her message and I thought, *who the hell would enjoy that?* She has every right to not love cleaning up someone else's bodily fluids at 4 a.m., even if it is part and parcel of the whole motherhood gig. Just because something is in the job description doesn't mean it's necessarily anyone's favorite part of the job.

In the beginning, I felt so guilty about not being the type of mother who enjoyed every minute. I'd see pictures of someone else's perfect life splashed across Facebook or Instagram and think, "I guess she's got this motherhood thing figured out." New to parenthood, I had little evidence of how other people raised their children, and those seemingly perfect lives lead me to believe that I was the one doing it wrong. In time, I've learned how misleading those little snapshots of people's lives truly are. Social media often becomes more of a highlight reel than a comprehensive look at anyone's actual circumstances. It's easy to cherry pick the best moments, apply a flattering filter and crop them into little shareable squares that tell a true (but very small) part of an incomplete story. Those people with the always-smiling babies and the amazing family vacations are leaving out the parts that are less pleasant for mass consumption; the type of things my girlfriend and I were chatting about privately for that very reason.

I realize now that the people who say they truly enjoy every minute are either liars or anomalies. Motherhood is an always-on-duty, never-get-a-break kind of job; to me, loving every minute is just not statistically possible. Sometimes it's belly laughs and happy, smiling children who look great with the Amaro filter and sometimes it's angry, teething babies and disobedient toddlers who smear peanut butter on the dog. When it's good, it's really good. But when it's not so great, I think it's still OK to wish it were really good.

So, to answer my friend's question, no it's not bad to sometimes want to enjoy it more. It's just realistic.

Humbled

It was one of those mornings where the kids were both up considerably earlier than usual. I'd spent the past few hours exhausting my options for entertaining them—songs, Play-Doh, food, Netflix—and I was quickly running out of ideas. It was 10:00 a.m. Suddenly, I remembered the library books we'd checked out the previous afternoon that were currently sitting in the trunk of my car in the driveway. "Wanna read some books about trucks?" I asked Chase enthusiastically before hopping to my feet and walking to the storm door. With the baby in the front pack, still in my bathrobe and slippers, I shut the door behind me and hustled to the car to retrieve the library books.

Books in hand, I crossed the porch 16 seconds later to discover an alarming state of events: Chase had learned to lock the glass storm door in my absence. There I was, standing on the front porch watching my toddler through the glass, trying not to panic. If he'd locked the door, surely I could teach him to unlock it. He recently learned the word "stuck," so I endeavored to use that to my advantage.

"Mommy's stuck," I told him. "Can you turn the button?"

He reached up and manipulated the lock, but it takes three turns to unlock and he gave up after one. When I asked him again, he turned it back the other way, effectively undoing any progress he made the first time. For the next ten minutes we repeated this charade, with him unsuccessfully turning the lock and me begging him to stay near the door where I could see him. I knew that if he disappeared into the depths of our house I would have no way of stopping him from climbing the stairs or emptying the entire pantry onto the floor. (Note to self: yet another reason why baby proofing before two years old would've been a good idea.)

Our neighborhood is full of summer renters and nine-to-fivers, so on an early fall morning there was no one around to help me. All the windows were locked and my phone sat inside on the same table as the keypad for the garage, which was waiting for my husband to repair it. I had no way of getting to my child and he could run off any second and do God knows what inside.

After ten torturously long minutes that felt like hours, the mail truck came chugging around the corner. I ran down to the street, frantically flagging him down. I must've looked like a lunatic, running down the hill in what were clearly my pajamas with wild hair and a baby strapped to me. "Can I use your phone to call my husband?" I asked desperately. "My toddler locked me out of the house and my phone is inside with him." The mailman graciously handed over his phone, then turned off his truck and followed me up to the house. "Maybe I can help," he offered. As soon as Chase saw the stranger outside the door, he started backing away.

"Oh, I think I'm scaring him," the mailman said. "I'll just stay out of his sight while you call your husband." I punched Adam's number into the phone and got him on the second ring. After I explained the situation, I assumed he would freak out. I pictured him driving the half hour home and busting down the door. Or, at the very least, he'd demand to know why I left our toddler inside by himself in first place. My gut twisted as I waited for his response.

"Well is the car unlocked?" he asked nonchalantly. "Just use your garage door opener."

I just stood there for about 10 seconds in stunned silence. And then: "Uh. Ha. Right. OK. Bye."

I hung up, feeling like a prize idiot. All my terror and panic instantly evaporated, quickly to be replaced by red-cheeked embarrassment. How the hell had I not thought of that as I was racking my brain for solutions? Explaining the situation to the mailman, I handed his phone back and thanked him for his help. He retreated across the lawn, back to his truck, where he waited for me to get inside before returning to his route. Thankfully, we'd lived in our house for over a year and had never seen our mailman, so it was unlikely I'd be running into him anytime soon.

The next afternoon, my husband and I ventured out to attend an old friend's wedding. The groom, Brandon, and I graduated high school together and he'd worked with Adam at a couple different summer jobs, so we'd known him for a good portion of our lives. His mom raised him alone and worked nights as a nurse, which meant his house was a prime hangout spot for bored teenagers with access to booze (Brandon's hair started going gray in seventh grade, so by high school he looked much older than 21). Neither Adam nor I had seen him in years, but we were looking forward to catching up and celebrating his marriage while getting a break from our kids.

The ceremony took place at an old Catholic church. Promptly at 2:30, the processional began and, one by one, the bridesmaids came filing to the front of the church, followed by our friend's mother, on the arm of her long-time boyfriend. Then, the man I could only assume was our friend's father—we'd never met him growing up—came into view between the back doors of the church, ready to proceed down the aisle.

"Holy shit," I whispered to Adam.

"I don't think you're supposed to say 'shit' in church," Adam whispered back.

"I think that's the mailman from yesterday. Oh my God. Brandon's *father* is the mailman from yesterday."

I couldn't believe it. What are the freakin odds? I still wasn't entirely sure that it was actually him though. I was almost positive, but I needed confirmation. Later in the evening at the cocktail hour, when the groom came around to say hello, we made small talk and exchanged pleasantries, caught up on old memories between trips to the open bar. As we chatted, I kept trying to judge whether an appropriate amount of time had passed for me to ask my burning question.

"Is your dad a mailman?" I ventured, with my second free drink in hand.

He laughed and responded, "He's YOUR mailman. Your neighborhood is on his route."

Well, OK then. The mystery was solved; my friend's father was the mailman who had witnessed my panicked idiocy the day before. I could tell he didn't remember me though; at one point I was standing directly in front of him in the buffet line and he was none the wiser.

After a few more cocktails, bolstered by liquid courage, I decided to approach him to say thank you. "You probably don't recognize me; I look a little different today," I said, standing in front of him in a dress and heels, makeup on and hair straightened. He looked at me quizzically and then I saw the moment it clicked. He laughed and turned to his wife.

"This is the girl from yesterday," he said and she smiled in amused recognition.

"Oh you're the one with the little baby?" I had to laugh—clearly I had been their dinner table conversation the night before.

"Yup, that's me," I said. "I just wanted to say thank you for helping me in a moment of panic. I had no idea what to do."

"You seemed so calm," he responded. "I was kind of impressed."

I was surprised to hear I'd come off that way, since I'd been anything but. "Well I was really scared—and clearly not thinking straight. So thank you." We said our goodbyes and I spent the rest of the evening trying to avoid another awkward run-in with him as we both danced to "Shout" in opposite corners of the dance floor.

As I relayed this story to my mother in law the following day, she smiled with that, "I've-been-there" look in her eyes. "Isn't motherhood so humbling?" she asked me, amusement still in her voice. It was the perfect word to describe what I'd just experienced, what I've experienced on so many occasions in the short time I've been a mother. As I've come to learn firsthand, motherhood is just one giant fall from grace down a big ass, never-ending hill.

It's the moment a stranger approaches you in a store to let you know you have spit up down the back of your shirt and you've been wearing the same sweater since 6:00 the previous morning. It's when you finally get to use the bathroom for the first time in hours and a tiny but very loud person pries your legs apart yelling, "POOP!" for three whole minutes in a crowded public restroom. It's when your breastfeeding infant rips the nursing cover off at a dinner party and exposes your bare nipples to your friend's husband whom you just met 30 seconds ago.

Any illusions I had of being a relatively put-together, passably functional human being, motherhood has effectively dispelled. I am basically at the complete mercy of my children's temperaments and bodily functions with no hope of seeming like I know what I'm doing ever again. Thankfully, I'm confident it's not just me; motherhood doesn't discriminate. Beyoncé may seem like an untouchable, goddess-like icon, but I'd be willing to bet she's had spitup in her highly coveted cleavage at one point or another.

Even on the off chance that I, too, experience a brush with fame someday, I will still be the woman on her hands and knees in the supermarket scraping up the entire container of Teddy Grahams that her toddler saw fit to throw on the floor. If at some point in the far off future I become a bestselling author or solve the world's hunger crisis, I will still be the woman who once found a booger on her lip that did not belong to her. And no matter what the rest of the year holds for me, I will still be the woman whose mailman is getting an extra big tip at Christmas this year, all thanks to motherhood: the most humbling job on the planet.

Brotherly Bond

Chase is at the age when being made to sit still is something akin to torture. Not that I think it should be any other way; little boys aren't really designed to be idle. It's just not in their genetic makeup. I knew when we began looking for a new church after our move that, if we wanted him to attend with us, we'd have to find one with a) services that lasted no longer than the time it took to get to the letter F in the ABCs, or b) had a nursery where kids could go during the service. Since we couldn't seem to find any with services shorter than 10 minutes, we went with one that had a great nursery (and that we loved for all the other reasons you pick a church. But *priorities*).

The church nursery has a preschool classroom-feel, with low shelving containing all manner of toys and stuffed animals, an undersized table and chair set and a play kitchen stocked with all the latest in plastic food. When we arrived to drop off Chase for the first time he was instantly drawn in by the bucket of toy trains in the corner. He set to work playing—stacking one on top of the other and zooming them across the low pile carpet while making choo choo noises. We thought, *Well, this is easy*. We gave him a quick kiss, let him say goodbye to his baby brother who was sleeping in the front pack and told him we'd be back soon. Just as we reached the door he came barreling toward us with tears in his eyes and a full-blown meltdown threatening to escape his little body. It should be noted that Chase had never particularly cared whether we were nearby or not; he'd always been the independent type who was unfazed when Adam left for work every morning and didn't bat an eyelash if we took off for a date night. Since Sam's birth, however, he'd been clingier, wanting us close by more often. Still, we hadn't anticipated his reaction. The teacher assured us he'd be fine—I couldn't help but flash back to my days of teaching preschool when I'd think the lingering parents were only prolonging the agony—so we closed the door behind us and began retreating upstairs where the music had already started. Even through the door my son's guttural scream was deafening. Already overly sensitive to all the changes in his world since his brother's arrival, I wanted to just go back in, collect him and say, "Well, I guess we'll try this again in a few years." But I knew I had to let him learn to adapt without us.

We immersed ourselves in the songs upstairs while the baby dozed in the front pack. I was sure Chase was fine by then—it never took him more than a few minutes to calm down—so I let myself relax infinitesimally. "I think I'm going to go check on him," Adam whispered a few minutes later. He disappeared down the stairs just as the pastor started in on his sermon. A handful of minutes went by, then another handful. Adam still hadn't come back. I didn't want to leave in the middle of the sermon—it's a small church and I knew my exit would be disruptive—so I just waited. And then waited some more. "What's up?" I texted surreptitiously from the back row. No response. I knew then that Chase must've still been upset and Adam had to stay to comfort him. Finally the service ended and the baby and I made our way down to the nursery where we found Adam and Chase racing Matchbox cars across the floor. I noticed Chase was wearing a different shirt than the one I'd dressed him in that morning. "He threw up a little when he was crying," the teacher explained. "No big deal—we just swapped his shirt out for the one in his bag." I was totally at a loss; he'd never gotten that upset before when we left him anywhere. I hoped this wasn't the new normal.

Every Sunday after that, we'd bring him to the nursery, and every Sunday he'd scream and cry as we left. Inevitably, Adam would go to check on him a few minutes into the service and never come back. For almost two months my husband spent nearly the full 75 minutes of the church service in the nursery instead of upstairs with me. We didn't know what to do.

The nursery teachers, Adam and I racked our brains trying to come up with a solution. We tried sneaking out without saying goodbye—with disastrous results. We attempted having one of the teachers come get him as soon as we got into church instead of us taking him down and leaving him in the nursery. No go. "We're never going to be able to attend the service together," I lamented to Adam.

After a few months of attending church and never successfully leaving Chase in the nursery, the obvious answer whacked me upside the head. "We should try leaving Sam in the nursery, too," I told Adam. "Chase hates to be away from his brother. Maybe he's upset because all of us are leaving him at once."

The following Sunday we decided to give it a shot. Chase began to cry as soon as we started to leave. He knew how that particular story ended and he wasn't happy about it. "Sam is going to stay here with you," I explained. "Mommy and daddy will back in a little bit. Can you play here with your brother?" Chase nodded, though he was still crying and reaching for us as we left. "We'll give it a few minutes and then come back and check on him," I told the teacher.

After the first couple songs, I headed back to the nursery. I peeked through the window and there he was, playing happily with a Thomas the Train set while the teacher held Sam. I couldn't believe it. My idea had worked.

During the last few months of my pregnancy with Sam I'd experienced overwhelming guilt about giving Chase a sibling when he was still so young. The thought of him hating the new baby for taking our attention was stifling; it kept me awake at night (along with the heartburn) turning over all the potential scenarios in my mind. I worried more than once that we'd made an irreparable mistake and that the new baby's birth was about to disrupt the beautiful balance of our current family. At the time of his brother's arrival Chase was only 17 months old. He wasn't old enough to understand the transition from my growing belly to the baby in my arms or that the baby was a person whom he was expected to love. But, inexplicably, he did love Sam, almost instantaneously. He didn't make a big deal out of welcoming him into our family; it was just like he'd always been part of it.

I know their relationship will morph and change countless times throughout their lives; I have no illusions that it will stay as it is in this moment, when they're both still coming into their own and learning each other. Even now it looks different by the day. As Sam develops new abilities and cultivates a personality, Chase displays bouts of jealousy and impatience with him that foretell the inevitable future of their sibling dynamic.

I can already envision the toddler Sam will be a year from now, tailing behind his three-year-old brother who has no time to indulge Sam's desire to color or play trains. Then I picture the moment Sam spills on the pavement, still unsteady on his feet, and Chase rushes over to help him up and quiet his dramatic howling. I imagine a scene in which an ill-mannered punk is picking on Sam during recess and Chase, who is usually content to pretend he doesn't have an annoying little brother one grade below him, comes to his aid and defends Sam's honor. I see a possible future in which they're at the same party; a party where Chase has had too much to drink and is about to get into a car and drive home. Sam notices his brother's heightening intoxication, steers him to the car, delivers him home safely and ushers him into his bed before Adam and I find out what they've been up to that night.

I realize there will be years of slights and sucker punches and annoyed eye rolls mixed in with those redeeming instances of brotherly love. I'm sure there will be more than a few times I question the decision we made to have them so close in age, in the hopes that they would also grow up closely bonded. For better or worse, our choice made them a team. Whether they embrace the bond or resist it, their lives will be fused together for much of the foreseeable future. I can only hope that the connection they forged the very first day I introduced Chase to his little brother in the hospital room will remain strong and unflinching—a solid, unwavering connection that defies time and circumstance. I hope that, even when they hate each other, they still love each other, too. And I hope that, no matter what, they always stay each other's safe place the way they've been right from the start.

I Am a Great Mother

*I*f asked, I'd have no trouble at all producing a list of my shortcomings as a mother. I could probably rattle off twelve of them in less time than it takes my toddler to locate the most dangerous item in the room as soon as I put it down (which is about 2.5 seconds and a steak knife, in case you were wondering). My failures and inadequacies are always ready to spring from my lips at a moment's notice; I keep them stored behind my tongue, nestled in beside all the words I wish I had the courage to say to the woman with the unsolicited parenting advice in aisle five of the grocery store.

It's even easier to let them tumble from my mouth when someone else speaks of her own shortcomings. "I know what you mean," I commiserate. "I'm always so impatient with my kids. They deserve better than that." Or, "I really need to get a handle on cleaning my house. It's constantly filthy and I can't stay on top of anything." Giving voice to my perceived deficiencies is almost second nature to me now, so much so that I rarely give much thought to it. It's almost like it requires no effort at all. But the things I'm doing right as a mother? Those are so much harder to conjure up (and, by the way, nobody likes a braggart). So I keep them locked up tight, never speaking of them out loud or even letting myself think them.

I don't know when it became en vogue to be a Bad Mom, but I have certainly fallen victim to that unfortunate trend. Sometimes, it's about acknowledging it myself before someone else does. If I've done something that makes me feel like a less-than-stellar mom, at least I can be the one to say so instead of waiting for another person to point out my shortcomings. Other times, it's just something to say; another way to cut myself down at the knees.

Chase fell down at the playground when I was wasn't looking? *Bad mom.* I forgot about Sam's pediatrician appointment? *Bad mom.* I didn't pack enough wipes in the diaper bag? *Bad mom.* It's like it has become instinctual, almost automatic, for me to sum up any mistake I make with this catchall phrase.

Do you want to know the truth? I'm tired of pretending to be a Bad Mom. It doesn't help my kids, it doesn't help me and, when I really assess all the evidence, it's just plain untrue. I am a great mom in all the most important ways: I love my children fiercely; I would do almost anything to make them happy. I give over my time and energy and personal hygiene to them on a daily basis.

But I am also a great mom in the unglamorous ways that nobody talks about, the routine parts of mothering that everyone does and shouldn't really need acknowledgment for doing. Maybe it's time I gave myself recognition for those things too.

I am a great mother because I weather the dreaded grocery store trip every week to feed them, even as they're grabbing things off the shelves and eating all the merchandise before we can buy it. I made the incredible sacrifice of feeding them from my body, which is often a thankless job, but gave them a healthy start to their lives.

I am a great mother because I give baths and wipe syrup from their hands and change diapers all day long. I dress them in (relatively) clean clothes every day, take them to get haircuts when they can no longer see and clip their fingernails, usually without making them bleed.

I am a great mother because I share everything I own with them, including, but not limited to my body, my bed and half of all my meals. I take showers with them and let them use my shirtsleeve as a tissue; I give them my scarce body heat, the only towel that's not soggy and the last bite of pizza that I really want for myself.

I am a great mother because I know them like the back of my hand. My mind is a veritable card catalogue of information I've stored away about my children: their likes and dislikes, habits and preferences, excitements and fears. I know that Chase is afraid of bounce houses and can't stand the feel of shaving cream; that he loves anything drowned in tomato sauce and prefers his food cold. I am learning Sam a little at a time, watching him develop his own unique identity apart from his brother, separate from me.

I am a great mother because I am here, day in and day out, doing all the little things that are part of being someone's mother. I do them automatically, because they have to get done and I am the one who makes sure that they do, even if they go completely unnoticed and under-appreciated. I am a great mother because, without all the little things I do every day, the grocery lists would stay unwritten and the dirty knees would remain unwashed and the whole balance to each day would spin off-kilter. I am a great mother because I keep showing up, even when I'd really prefer to ignore the baby monitor and pull the covers back over my head.

I am a great mother. Period.

Please, Not a Daughter

As we exited the tiny exam room clutching the grainy, black-and-white evidence of a second baby boy, I nearly floated to the car, buoyed as I was by relief. "Are you sure?" my husband asked after the ultrasound technician pointed to the microscopic confirmation of our son's gender on the screen. She smiled and typed out "It's a BOY!" in bold yellow letters before printing off several copies for us to take home. I was shocked. For the entire 18 weeks preceding the appointment I'd carried an unshakeable belief that this second baby was a girl. I'd even gone so far as to refer to my belly as a "she" and had used the term "sister" when explaining the idea of a sibling to my older son. So much for mother's intuition.

Most people were surprised by my reaction. Surely I longed for floral patterned dresses and thick hair to braid, patent leather shoes and sparkly pink fingernails? Didn't I want a daughter to whom I could pass down my wedding dress? A little girl who would play dress up in my heels? A companion to someday discuss men and menstrual cycles and child rearing? My answer to all of that was a firm *no*. I reasoned that boys are simpler, less complicated. They make sense to me in a way that girls do not. They invite less drama and forgive more readily. Plus, I had rooms full of boy stuff already—no need to start stockpiling an endless supply of pastel-colored princess garb.

But the real reason I was relieved had nothing to do with any of that.

For six years I suffered from a life-altering eating disorder. My mind was not my own. My thoughts were consumed completely by food and weight: avoiding, gaining, bingeing, covering up. I went to great lengths to further my addiction and hide my disease, including cutting people out of my life before they could get close enough to discover my secret. Those six years were the loneliest of my life.

The process of losing myself to my eating disorder was far more gradual than some would suspect. An inch here, a pound there. Fifteen extra minutes at the gym. Then thirty extra minutes. Then ninety. I didn't set out with a goal of losing 25 pounds or shrinking my waist four inches. In fact, I didn't intend for any of it to happen. I started naturally losing weight and quickly became addicted to the high. Looking back, it's almost as if it was fated, like I was somehow predisposed to falling down the rabbit hole of mental illness. That's the part that scares the shit out of me.

Before things got bad, I'd been happy. Confident. Comfortable in my own skin. I was 17 on the warm October night when the Red Sox won their first World Series in 86 years— less than a year from when my problems began—and I showed up to school with my entire face painted bright red. I was bold. Interesting. I had moxie. Until I didn't anymore.

If it was that easy for me to slip away, how would my own daughter fare? I could give her all the positive affirmation in the world but if my faulty genetic makeup predisposed her to self-hatred, I'd be no better equipped to save her than I'd been to save myself.

I don't worry about that with my boys, and maybe that's shortsighted. It's possible they show their insecurities differently than women. I'm sure there are men with body image hang-ups, ones like the guy lifting weights beside me at the gym, flexing and preening in the mirror. But the statistics don't lie: body image is not nearly the same problem for a man as it is for his female counterpart.

The reason I've never worried about Chase and Sam struggling with body image has more to do with my husband than with the statistics. I've encountered few people more at ease in their own skin than Adam. It's not just the physical aspect, though he's always carried himself in such a way that you can tell he feels at home in his body. More than that, he is truly comfortable being exactly who he is, no matter the audience or the circumstance. He doesn't put on airs or try to mold his personality so that others will like him. He just is—take him or leave him.

As long as I've known Adam, he's radiated a quiet confidence that's neither arrogant nor showy. He's not self-involved or a braggart. He just truly likes himself, without apologizing for it. My mother-in-law once told me that when Adam was a kid, most of his classmates considered him their best friend. It didn't matter whether or not he thought any of them were *his* best friend— that natural ease and confidence has always made people want to align themselves with him. He's the guy people put down as a job reference, the one always picked to be in friends' wedding parties. His self-assurance is a magnetizing force.

When I look at Chase, I see that quality developing in him already. My mother-in-law tells me how much he reminds her of a young Adam all the time. Most of the moms I know search their children's features and habits hoping to see themselves in the mix, but not me. I'm relieved that my older son is nothing like me so far. It gives me hope that Adam's genetics will muscle mine out in the fight for Chase's budding personality. I'm more than happy to let his win.

But a girl? A girl would be at a disadvantage from the start. The world is often unkind to women, especially those who are prone to weakness. It preys on fragilities and exploits perceived shortcomings. Even if I armored my daughter in confidence and strength, my genetics could still turn out to be her Achilles' heel—the one vulnerability she never expected until it was too late.

The first time I'd witness her standing before the full-length mirror pinching her waist, the burden of my guilt would break me. The moment I'd watch her pass up a slice of cake at a friend's birthday party because she'd begun to take notice of her slightly rounder belly, my remorse would eat me alive. I would know that, despite my best efforts, I had a hand in laying the path she walked to get to that point. I'm not sure my heart could take it.

We do not yet know whether a third child will join our family someday. The two boys are enough to keep us plenty busy for the foreseeable future. But there is always that question mark lingering in my mind: What if, years from now, the ultrasound technician points to the screen and the news is exactly what I've feared all this time? Would my nurturing be enough to keep my daughter from wandering down the same path I walked? Or would nature take the wheel instead? I'd have no way of predicting what the future held for her. That's what scares me the most.

If and when the time comes for us to add another member to our brood, I know most of our family and friends will be hoping for a girl. They'll want to shower her with pretty bows and pink tutus, help think up cutesy nicknames. They'll size up my belly and declare that it must be a girl, just look at the way I'm carrying this time. And all the while, I'll be there amidst the loud predictions and proclamations, quietly praying for one last son.

Settling Down

I am not a patient person. The trait seems to have been omitted from my genetic makeup entirely, a missing link among my DNA strands. It has been a problem as long as I can remember; even as a child, I was constantly rushing. Though I adored reading, I would hurry through books I loved for the sole purpose of getting to the end. Then, once I finally finished, I'd feel disappointed and bereft, wishing I'd savored the words a little more along the way.

Part of me blames my father for this genetic shortcoming. Impatience is sort of his thing. Not in a mean or careless way—he doesn't cut people off when they're talking or half-ass tasks in order to reach the end more quickly—just in the sense that he's constantly looking toward whatever is coming next. As a kid I found the habit endlessly exciting. He always had grand plans for the future, some big idea that we could finally put into motion once something changed or enough time had passed.

His enthusiasm for what lay ahead was catching. I found my-self often wanting to speed up time just to get to the next ad-venture: the family vacation penciled on the calendar in July, Christmas with my rarely-seen cousins, the day I could finally drive myself to school or stay out past 10:00 with my boyfriend. In many cases, the anticipation swelled so large in my head that the actual event, when it finally came, was something of a let-down. I invested so much in the idea of the future that I found myself enjoying the present just a little less.

In high school, I eschewed parties and school functions; I skipped out on my senior prom and kept an entire spiral-bound notebook full of countdowns to college. My boyfriend (who is now my husband) graduated two years before me and I was hell-bent on getting out of high school and into the real world as soon as possible.

The novelty of college wore off quickly, however. By sopho-more year, I'd already decided to cut my five-year program down to four in order to graduate faster and join the working world. I secured a good job at the company where I'd interned through-out college during a time when the recession was looming large and jobs were scarce—especially for new graduates—but within a month was already saying goodbye to the position in favor of moving two states away to be with Adam. I knew I'd settle down and stop rushing once we finally lived together and started creat-ing a life for ourselves. Everything would be complete then—what reason would I have to wish it away in favor of the next thing?

After eight long years apart, we finally married, bought a house and had the pleasure of waking up next to each other every morning. Our finances and laundry merged; he tried couscous for the first time and I had someone to warm up my perpetually cold feet in bed at night. It felt like domestic bliss. Except for that one tiny, nagging thought that took up residence in the back corner of my mind: children. I was barely 23 when we got married and yet I was looking to tick that big life event off my list. I didn't understand how to settle down.

Thankfully, we gave ourselves a few years to be a couple before we decided to start trying for a family. All the while, anytime I began to feel a little nauseous or had a random unexplained ache, I'd sprint to the nearest drugstore and throw away $20 on a package of pregnancy tests. *Maybe it'll just happen*, I reasoned, *and I won't have to wait*. Needless to say, I wasted a lot of perfectly good beer money on single blue lines.

When I got pregnant at 26, I was elated. No more waiting. I finally had what I really wanted, the life I'd dreamt of so often during the years Adam and I spent apart. I just needed to get past the first trimester with the all-day sickness, bloated midsection and voracious post-midnight appetite. Once I finally looked pregnant instead of like I'd eaten a few too many cheeseburgers, I'd savor the miracle happening inside me. But then the second trimester came and I found myself cheating the numbers. I'd tell people I was 14 weeks along when I was really 13; I booked my anatomy scan as early as the obstetrical office would allow so I could hurry up and find out whether we were having a boy or girl. Throughout the entire third trimester, I reasoned that I was big and uncomfortable and I just wanted to meet our baby already; of course it was normal for me to want to hit fast forward. On and on it went, even after my first son was born. Nine months after we brought him home from the hospital, I was pregnant again by choice. Settling down was not in my wheelhouse.

The other morning, as I do several times a day, I was helping Chase down the stairs. He's almost old enough to navigate them by himself but not with total confidence. It's one of the few tasks for which he still requests my aid. As he meandered down them ever so slowly, I found myself pulling at his hand while he stopped to admire the dust bunnies gathered on the stair and then decided to plop down and have a rest after only four steps. "C'mon, bud," I prompted, with an impatient edge creeping into my voice. "Quick like a bunny." The phrase harkens back to my preschool teaching days and I find myself using it often, a knee jerk reaction to my son's painstakingly slow progression down the stairs or across a parking lot when I'm juggling his brother and an arm full of grocery bags. It's basically a cutesy way of saying *hurry the hell up*. In this case, there was none of the danger of a parking lot, no grocery bags threatening to spill across the driveway and, in all honesty, absolutely nowhere we had to be once he finally descended the stairs. So why the hell was I rushing him?

The same reason I rushed through his newborn phase, wanting to push past the age of floppy necks and angry nighttime howls: I truly couldn't wait for what came next.

"I can't wait until he's able to smile at us," I'd remark to my husband, gazing wistfully at our emotionless newborn. "Won't that be so gratifying?"

Then as he got older: "I can't wait until he's really feeding himself. It'll be so much easier when we don't have to spoon feed him everything."

And once he became a mischievous toddler: "I can't wait until he's old enough to be alone in a room for more than 12 seconds without having to worry he'll set fire to the house. That will be so nice."

It was always something. There was always some reason that the current phase wasn't quite satisfying enough, but that the next phase would meet all the right criteria.

Last year, about a week before Christmas, I had to run into the drugstore around the corner from our house to pick up a few items. The streets and shops surrounding the store were decked out in twinkly lights and inflatable Santas, plastic nativity scenes and pointy-toed elves. Basically it was the way the world is supposed to look a week before Christmas. But inside the store the displays were unexplainably crammed with Valentine's Day fare: teddy bears clutching embroidered "Be Mine" hearts and bouquets of fake red roses, bags of sugary pink candies and rows upon rows of gaudily wrapped Russell Stover chocolates. All the Christmas merchandise had already been relegated to a single shelf in the back corner of the store, procrastinators be damned.

The scene struck a chord of annoyance in me. Christmas hadn't even been celebrated yet (truth be told, I'd yet to finish my shopping) and already we were expected to move onto the next holiday. *Why can't we just slow the hell down and enjoy what's happening right now instead of pushing forward to the next thing?* I wondered. *It's going to come anyway, so what's the use in rushing it?*

I didn't recognize the significance of my own questioning; I was just ticked off at the advertising industry for steamrolling my favorite holiday. Until I really thought about it, I didn't consider that the corporate head honcho behind all that rushing was probably a person exactly like me. A person who *just can't wait* for the next thing to come along.

During my second pregnancy I was a mess of emotions. At certain times, I was dying to reach the end and at others determined to soak it all in. I wasn't sure whether or not it was the last pregnancy and, if it happened to be, I wanted to cherish every detail. Yet with all the scares and complications I'd experienced, I also wanted him on the outside, where I'd at least know he was safe from what I once believed was an imminent and devastating end to my pregnancy.

Now that he's here a strange thing is happening. I've become desperate for time to slow down, even stop. It is the complete opposite of my attitude during Chase's first year. Recognizing that this could well be the last of all the firsts, I am frantic in my attempt to avoid wishing it away. I want to be present. Patient. Grateful. But, as if the universe is mocking me for all the rushing I've done up until now, the passage of time has only seemed to double in speed rather than halt at my urging. It's a cruel punishment, one that I probably deserve. Just when I'd be content to linger in the same phase indefinitely, time has a much different plan.

"Stay this little forever, OK?" I jokingly demand of Chase as he stands before the easel, sizing up his masterpiece with an adorably furrowed brow. This time my question is lighthearted and playful, matching his current mood. He replies with a flippant yes, the answer he gives when he recognizes the way a question turns up at the end but is one he doesn't quite understand. Other times, my pleas are more fervent, desperate even. "Please don't grow up," I implore Sam as he lies draped across my upper half, the melodic rhythm of his snores filling my ear. I am no longer thinking about the future version of him; the one who will career through the yard on the heels of his older brother next summer. I am only thinking of the baby he is now, the one who still needs me—only me—to nurse him to sleep. I take his silence as a tacit agreement to remain this small indefinitely and find comfort in the irrationality.

For once, I can wait to find out what the future holds for us. For once, I find comfort in the here and now. For once, I am watching our lives play out in real time rather than constantly hitting the fast forward button. After all this time, I am finally settling down.

Cheers to the Mamas

Cheers to the mamas-to-be for whom nine months feels like eternity. The ones who are quietly puking in trash cans under their desks, trying to hide their little secret from their nosy coworkers. The ones for whom everything is an occasion to cry, including Campbell's soup commercials and YouTube videos of dogs making friends with koala bears and the rising number on the scale at the doctor's office. The ones who stopped shaving their legs four months ago and really don't give a fuck if their husbands mind. The ones who have glowing skin and a little round bump under a cute maternity dress whom everyone secretly wants to chuck off a bridge.

Cheers to the breastfeeding mamas who are making such a sacrifice for their children. The ones whose nipples are cracked and bleeding and feel like a little piranha is gnawing on them 22 out of 24 hours every day. The ones who are a slave to the pump and cannot wait to unplug for all eternity. The ones who are successfully nursing big, healthy beautiful babies and are proud of their accomplishment.

Cheers to the formula feeding mamas who are healthfully feeding their babies despite criticism and judgment from others. The ones who can't or chose not to breastfeed but don't feel that it's anyone else's business. The ones who are paying an arm and a leg for the nutrients that are making their babies healthy and strong.

Cheers to the women who want so badly to be mamas, the ones who are drowning in ovulation kits and hormone shots and negative pregnancy tests, just waiting for the day those two little lines will make their appearance. The ones who are buried in adoption papers and red tape and social worker phone calls, hoping one day they'll get to bring their child home.

Cheers to the mamas of newborns who are just barely hanging on. The ones who count four-hour stretches of sleep as something akin to heaven. The ones who haven't showered in two (three?) days, whose hairdresser would cry if she got a glimpse of them. The ones who accidentally "forgot" to tell their husbands that the doctor gave them the green light three weeks ago.

Cheers to the stay-at-home mamas who are on duty all day. The ones who plan activities and listen to inane music on repeat and wash the floor at naptime while simultaneously folding the sixth load of laundry. The ones whom everyone else thinks is getting manicures and taking naps and eating lots of chocolate covered things. The ones who feel endlessly guilty for not contributing to the household finances and are always trying to prove exactly what they did all day when people inevitably ask.

Cheers to the working mamas who are out there showing their children what balance and hard work looks like. The ones who feel fulfilled by their jobs, but wish they could be in two places at once; the ones who hate their jobs, but need the money; the ones who basically sign away their paycheck to daycare every Friday. The ones who worked their asses off for their degree or the position at their job and feel like they can't just walk away from all that time and effort and mountain of student loan debt. The ones who have dishes waiting and dinner to make and quality time to spend with their babies all in the hour-and-a-half before bedtime. The ones who cry when the nanny tells them about another first that they missed.

Cheers to the seasoned mamas who so totally got this mama thing down. The ones pushing double BOB strollers with one kid strapped to their chest while drinking a pumpkin spice latte and walking the family dog. The ones who can pack three lunches in 30 seconds flat: one for the gluten-free kid, one with an extra cheese stick, one with absolutely no tree nuts, *thankyouverymuch*. The ones who are at every soccer practice and preschool parent-teacher conference and car wash fundraiser when they'd really rather be sitting at home in the dark doing absolutely nothing while no one asks one single question about what the moon is made of and where babies come from.

Cheers to the single mamas whose spouse isn't right around the corner to relieve them after a long day. The ones who have to be both mom and dad, who are on duty every minute of every day without reprieve, who are solely responsible for everything under the sun. They are the readers of every bedtime story, the packers of every lunch, the dropper-offers and the picker-uppers. They are the ones who wonder if they'll ever find the perfect man to be both father and husband, especially when dating is almost impossible with absolutely no free time. They are the ones I consider braver and stronger than almost any other mama I can think of.

Cheers to you who is doing the best she knows how even when the kitchen floor is sticky and the permission slip is unsigned and everything's not perfect. You got this, mama.

Acknowledgements

First of all, I have to thank The Big Guy Upstairs, because without Him, none of this would be possible. The circumstances in my life were not at all conducive to writing a book, so I have to believe He nudged me down this (crazy) path with good reason. For that, I am eternally grateful.

For the OMTA mamas, I have nothing but love and gratitude. Not only have you allowed me to share my life with you through my writing, but you've shared yours with me as well. So many of these stories contain pieces of each of you and all the wisdom you've bestowed on me over the past couple years. Thank you for supporting me, encouraging me and teaching me as I learned how to be a mother.

My deepest gratitude goes out to my editor, Jennifer Oradat, who took my words and made them that much better. Your book baby is off to kindergarten now!

I would also like to thank my writer friends who supported me, cheered me on, proofread drafts, weighed in on cover designs, offered wisdom and generally tolerated me throughout the process of writing this book. Writing is a lonely profession and I would never be able to survive it without people in my corner who understand what a labor of love it is to birth a book.

I would be remiss if I didn't thank my parents, Keith and Judy Kenyon, for nurturing my love of the written word from a young age and supporting me every day of this journey thereafter.

I'll never be able to adequately express how thankful I am for my husband, Adam, whose ceaseless support and belief in me knows no bounds. All the nights you wrangled the kids into bed so I could write in peace and the many times when I told you, "I just have to finish this one little thing!" and two hours would go by, you were helping make my dream come true. I love you and the life we've created together. Thank you for giving me the courage to chase down my crazy dreams.

And, last but certainly not least, I have to thank my boys, Chase and Sam. Even after writing a whole book about being your mother, I will still never be able to capture in words the depth of my love for you. But I tried anyway.

About the Author

Rhode Island-based writer Melissa Mowry is the voice behind the popular blog, One Mother to Another, where she chronicles modern day challenges in parenthood with wit and heart. Her work has been featured on many popular websites including The Huffington Post and Scary Mommy, and she's been named one of the Funniest Parents on Facebook by TODAY Parents. Melissa resides in the Ocean State with her husband and their two boys. For more information, visit her website www.one-mother-to-another.com.

Hey there,

Thank you so much for buying a copy of *One Mother to Another*. If you enjoyed it, please consider leaving a review on Amazon or recommending it to a friend. Positive reviews and word of mouth recommendations are the lifeblood of this book and help ensure more moms will hear about it!

Gratefully yours,
Melissa